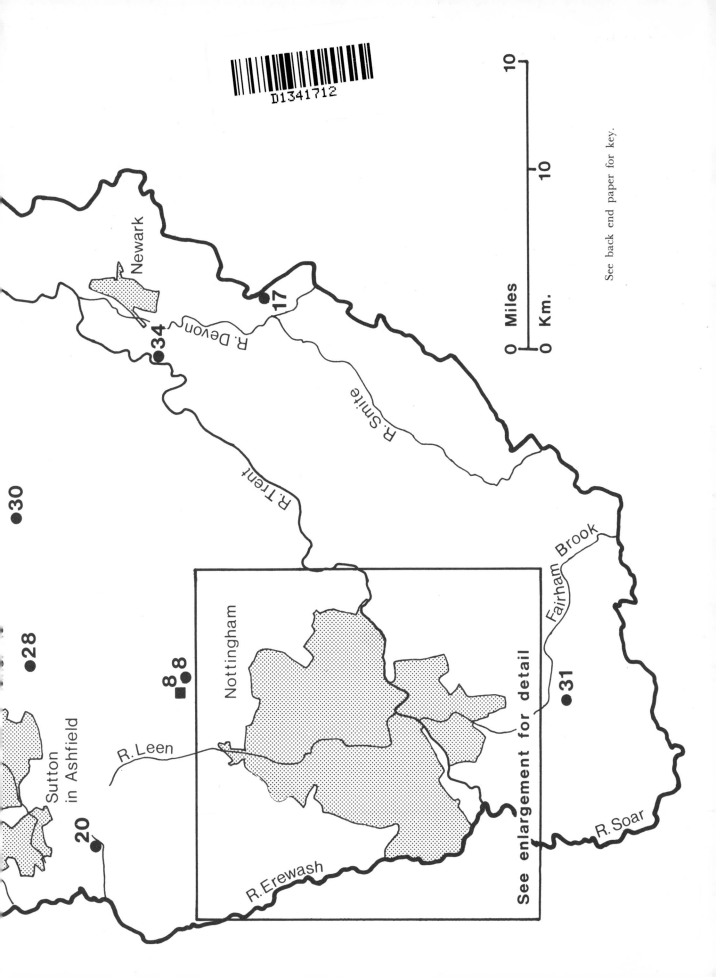

The Nature of Nottinghamshire 1987
has been published in a
Limited Edition
of which this is

Number

A list of subscribers
is printed at the
back of the book

THE NATURE OF
NOTTINGHAMSHIRE

THE NATURE OF NOTTINGHAMSHIRE

THE WILDLIFE AND ECOLOGY
OF THE COUNTY

EDITED BY
RICHARD MARQUISS

Cover illustration by
GRAHAME SMITH

Drawings by
KEN MESSOM & WOL EATON

Text contributed by
RICHARD MARQUISS, BRIAN PLAYLE, LAWRENCE BEE, EIRLYS GILBERT,
NICK MYHILL, AUSTEN DOBBS, DAVID TYLDESLEY, SUSAN PAGE,
JACK RIELEY, DEREK WARREN AND BRIAN WETTON

Principal photographs by
MARTIN AND DOROTHY GRACE, DERICK SCOTT, DEREK WARREN, JOHN FISHER,
MICHAEL BARKE, R.H. HALL, DAVID SMITH AND SARAH MONTGOMERY

Published with the co-operation and in aid of
THE NOTTINGHAMSHIRE TRUST
FOR NATURE CONSERVATION

FOREWORD BY SIR DAVID ATTENBOROUGH CBE, FRS

BARRACUDA BOOKS LIMITED
BUCKINGHAM, ENGLAND
MCMLXXXVII

THE NATURE OF BRITAIN SERIES

PUBLISHED BY BARRACUDA BOOKS LIMITED
BUCKINGHAM, ENGLAND
AND PRINTED BY
M & A THOMSON LITHO LTD
GLASGOW, SCOTLAND

BOUND BY
HUNTER & FOULIS LTD
EDINBURGH, SCOTLAND

COLOUR PLATES AND JACKETS BY
CHENEY & SONS LTD
BANBURY, OXON

MONOCHROME LITHOGRAPHY BY
FORE COLOUR GRAPHICS
HERTFORD, ENGLAND

COLOUR LITHOGRAPHY BY
WESTFIELD STUDIO LIMITED
ABINGDON, ENGLAND

TYPESET BY
QUILL AUTOGRAPHICS LIMITED
BANBURY, ENGLAND

©The Nottinghamshire Trust for Nature Conservation Limited 1987

All rights reserved. No part of the publication may be reproduced, stored
in a retrieval system, or transmitted, in any form or by any means,
electronic, mechanical, photocopying, recording or otherwise without the
prior permission of Barracuda Books Limited.

Any copy of this book issued by the Publisher as clothbound or as a
paperback is sold subject to the condition that it shall not by way or trade
or otherwise, be lent, re-sold, hired out or otherwise circulated without the
Publisher's prior consent, in any form of binding or cover other than that
in which it is published, and without a similar condition including this
condition being imposed on a subsequent purchaser.

ISBN 0 86023 277 8

Contents

List of Colour Plates

Tawny owl. (WE)

Foreword

by Sir David Attenborough CBE, FRS

If a stranger sitting next to you on an aeroplane, as you drone from one continent to another, asks you where you come from and your answer is Nottinghamshire, the response you will get (unless your questioner is a fellow-native) is likely to be one of polite disinterest or even bafflement. Nottinghamshire after all, has no spectacular mountains, no picturesque coasts, no vast and dramatic swamps. Its landscape is gentle, its beauties subtle and not easily yielded to those who rush through it on their way to some more publicised and glamourised vista. It is, however, the geographical centre of England and to those of us who know it, it is England's very heart.

I cannot boast that I am a true Nottinghamshire man for, owing to a temporary aberration on my parents' part, I was born not beside the Trent but the Thames. I do, however, bear the name of a Nottinghamshire village and both my father and my mother were born within a few miles of it. So I maintain that, in my genes as well as in my surname, I belong to Nottinghamshire.

The woods where, as a boy, I watched birds and foxes, the hillsides and river banks where I collected fossils, the ponds where I fished for tadpoles and newts were, to be pedantically accurate, just beyond the southern boundary of the county in Leicestershire, but ecologically they were virtually identical to many of those described in the pages of this book. Such delectable places, as everyone knows, are becoming fewer and fewer, year by year and month by month. No one can claim, least of all someone from the Midlands, that the English countryside should be protected from the hand of man. It has been made by man. The hedgerows, the gravel pits, the grassy ramparts of Iron Age camps around the hill-tops, the hummocked meadows that in medieval times were open strip-fields, the spinneys and the coppiced coverts, all these are man-made and the fact that they are so brings not dismay but added pleasure to anyone with the least historical imagination. Indeed, the actions of the human population of the county, over the past two thousand years, have not reduced but increased the diversity of its habitats and therefore of its flora and fauna. It is precisely this diversity that is a measure of the county's natural treasures and we should be doing everything we can to ensure that it is maintained, undiminished, for the delight of generations to come.

No one knows the countryside better than those people who live in it. No one understands better than they why and how it should be protected. Such people are, these days, gathered together in the County Trusts for Nature Conservation. Nationally the forty eight Trusts in the United Kingdom, through the association to which they all belong, the Royal Society for Nature Conservation, are at last making their voice heard in Westminster and wherever else decisions are being taken that affect the countryside. Individually, each Trust gives special protection and care to its own county. This invaluable, thoughtful and knowledgeable book, written by members of the Nottinghamshire Trust, is a magnificent example of the enterprise and expertise that the Trusts can deploy. It will, I am sure, be a revelation to many who before had been unaware of the natural riches of this lovely county, and so serve as a powerful incentive to all of us to cherish and protect them. I wish it every success.

David Attenborough

Little ringed plovers. (WE)

Key to Caption Credits
PHOTOGRAPHERS

MB	Michael Barke	SM	Sarah Montgomery
BC	British Coal	NEP	*Nottingham Evening Post*
BVC	B.V. Case	NCC	Nottinghamshire County Council
JC	John Crocker	NTNC	Notts Trust 'archives'
JF	John Fisher	SP	Susan Page
AG	Anthony Gough	DS	Derick Scott
M&DG	Martin and Dorothy Grace	STWA/VH	Severn Trent Water Authority/Valerie Holt
RHH	R.H. Hall	D Sm	David Smith
AL	Antoni Lachetta	JW	John Warham
NL	Norman Lewis	DW	Derek Warren
JLM	J.L. Mason	SW/NNHM	Sheila Wright/Nottingham Natural History Museum
HM	Hugh Miller		

ARTISTS

WE	Wol Eaton	KM	Ken Messom

FRONT COVER
GS   Grahame Smith

Introduction

This book has been written and illustrated by a team of busy people from a variety of backgrounds who are, nevertheless, united by their commitment to the wildlife of their county. Each has brought his or her own particular knowledge, experience and interest to bear upon the chapter to which he or she has contributed. No rigid adherence to style or approach was demanded. The result is as various and distinctive, and we hope pleasing, as the wildlife and countryside that it sets out to celebrate.

From the very beginning it was decided that this would not be an account of a countryside mysteriously emptied of human beings. The influence of people upon the nature of Nottinghamshire has been far too pervasive for that. Consequently, throughout the book, but particularly perhaps in the long woodland chapter and the Dukeries chapter, human and natural history have been interwoven in just the kind of relationship that has formed our modern countryside, and the place that wild nature has within it.

We hope, above all, that this will be a book to be looked at, read and enjoyed as a faithful and affectionate portrayal of the nature of Nottinghamshire. In its pages will be found most of the familiar, and some of the unfamiliar places where plants and animals remain to delight us; along the banks of the Trent, in the leafy depths of Robin Hood's green wood, in the productive environment created by gravel workings or in quiet corners of our busy towns. However, we also hope that our readers will be encouraged to become Nottinghamshire's defenders as well as its admirers. Our wildlife is under threat from many quarters and needs the active help of us all. With this in mind, the book has also been written to help celebrate the 1988 Silver Jubilee of the Nottinghamshire Trust for Nature Conservation. Outside the writing and illustrating team, many other individuals and organisations have been generous with their assistance. These include Allen Edwards, John Morgan, John McMeeking, Judith Marquiss, various sections of the Nottinghamshire County Council, the Severn-Trent Water Authority and the Meteorological Office/Nottingham Weather Centre. The diagrams were drawn by Martin Roberts. Martin and Dorothy Grace worked wonders in producing black and white prints from their original coloured slides. Throughout, Norman Lewis has provided many wise words of advice and guidance to the Editor. The kind support of innumerable other members of the Trust is also acknowledged.

We are grateful to Hodder and Stoughton for permission to quote from Arthur Mee's *The King's England: Nottinghamshire* and to Michael Joseph and the Rainbird Publishing Group Ltd for their agreement for us to use some material from *The New Shell Guide to England*.

We are also particularly grateful to Sir David Attenborough who managed to find time in his busy schedule to write the Foreword. This is by no means his first gesture of support for nature conservation in Nottinghamshire and we thank him warmly.

With so much ground to cover and so many facts to check and check again, some errors in the book will no doubt be discovered by the eagle-eyed. For these I take full responsibility and would welcome any correction that may be forthcoming.

The opinions expressed in the book are the writers' own and are not necessarily those of the Nottinghamshire Trust for Nature Conservation.

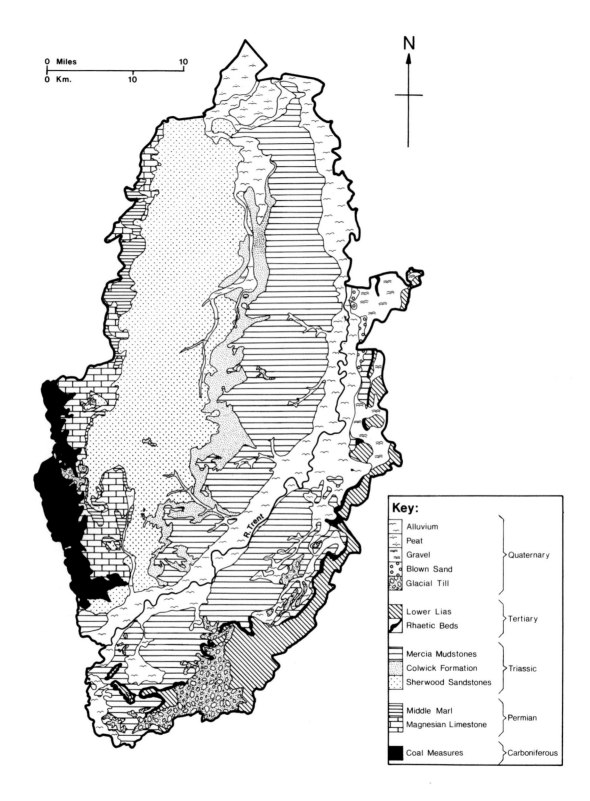

Key:

Alluvium	
Peat	
Gravel	Quaternary
Blown Sand	
Glacial Till	
Lower Lias	
Rhaetic Beds	Tertiary
Mercia Mudstones	
Colwick Formation	Triassic
Sherwood Sandstones	
Middle Marl	
Magnesian Limestone	Permian
Coal Measures	Carboniferous

A simplified geological map of Nottinghamshire.

12

A Background to Nottinghamshire

(KM)

'Nottinghamshire is a long oval shape rather suggestive of a big sand-grouse's egg' wrote Joseph Whitaker, one of the county's best-known natural historians in 1907. Later on in his account of the birds of Nottinghamshire, Whitaker dourly informs his readers that 'The county is on the whole mainly corn and turnip land . . .'. Even Arthur Mee, himself a Nottinghamshire man born in Stapleford, seems reluctant to get too excited in his 1938 *King's England* guide to the county, calling it 'truly a midland county, an average piece of this green and pleasant land'. The aim of this opening chapter is to go beyond these rather guarded descriptions and provide a fuller picture of the county in terms of some of its physical, social and historical characteristics. Without some insight into the shape and structure of an area, and the way in which the activities of man have impinged upon its landscape, an understanding of the local wildlife will be, at best, incomplete. The nature of Nottinghamshire is the product of a mixture of complex ingredients, which have combined in a unique way to provide us with the rich variety of plants and creatures which will unfold in subsequent chapters. Nottinghamshire is a county described variously as belonging to the East or to the North Midlands. Bounded by Derbyshire in the west, Yorkshire in the north, Lincolnshire in the east and Leicestershire in the south, it covers 216,365 hectares (534,638 acres). It is very much a lowland county, with between a third and two fifths lying below an altitude of 30 metres (100 feet). The highest point of just over 200 metres (660 feet) is in the Huthwaite area in the west of the county. Its position provides a gentle (if by no means uniform) descent from the southern Pennines to the lower-lying ground towards East Anglia. An outstanding and dominant feature of the landscape is the River Trent, which drains virtually the whole of Nottinghamshire. It enters the county in the south-west near Attenborough, flows past Nottingham and Newark and leaves in the north-east. For its final section, between Dunham and West Stockwith, it forms the county boundary with Lincolnshire. The valley of the Trent has played a central part in the lives—human and animal—of the inhabitants of Nottinghamshire. Overall, there is little spectacular scenery in the county, but its quiet and subtly various landscape provides much to admire and enjoy. Its central position, being about 160 kilometres (100 miles) from the west coast and 112 kilometres (70 miles) from the east, makes it very much a county at the green heart of England. An essential part of the background of any county is its underlying geology. Nottinghamshire, like many other English shires, has had a chequered and eventful geological history stretching back several hundred million years. Jungles, swamps, desert plains, shallow seas and even glaciers have, at different times, played their part in moulding the present landscape. This fascinating story is captured in the geological map of the county. Here, a pattern of bands is seen broadly lying in a north-south direction. Each of these bands represents sediments laid down in a particular geological environment during successive episodes of geological time. A traveller journeying from the Derbyshire border in an easterly or south-easterly direction and crossing these bands is travelling up the geological timescale, from older to increasingly younger sediments or rocks.

The oldest rocks are those of the Coal Measures exposed on the surface along the Nottinghamshire-Derbyshire border. The hard sandstones and soft shales of the Coal Measures on the eastern flank of the River Erewash have been eroded to form small hills and vales. These were the sediments formed in huge swamps which covered much of the Midlands about 300 million years ago. The fact that these muddy swamps often supported luxuriant vegetation, which died and became buried and compacted to form layers of coal, meant that this western part, from medieval times, has been an important coal-producing area. The Coal Measures are succeeded to the east by a modest ridge of up to eight kilometres (five miles) wide, and from 153-183 metres (500-600 feet) high, which stretches northwards from Nottingham eventually to Northumberland along a line often shared by the M1 motorway. This ridge represents the sandy limestones (Magnesian Limestone) and marls of the Permian rocks, which provide the present-day county with its only areas of craggy scenery. With the demise of the Coal Measure forest swamps the scene was set, about 250 million years ago, for the incursion of an inland sea, so salty that probably little life existed in it. Bulwell lies on the approximate line of its southernmost shore, and the buff-coloured sandy and dolomitic limestones of the Nottingham area can be traced to Mansfield and further north, where the traditional Mansfield White Sandstone and Red Sandstone, in reality sandy limestones, have provided building stone and, more recently, construction aggregate.

Travelling further east into the Nottingham heartland, the Sherwood Sandstone (formerly known as Bunter Sandstone) country is reached. This takes us back to about 240 million years ago, when Nottinghamshire was part of an extensive delta network, with mighty rivers from the south-west disgorging vast quantities of sand and pebbles in much the same way as the River Mississippi does today. In modern times the exposed sandstone formed from these ancient deltas breaks down to give a dry, poor and light, pebbly soil susceptible to windblow. It is not surprising that the traditional Sherwood Forest, with its glades of oaks and birches and tracts of open heathland, should have developed in this area. An important role played since about 1850 by the sandstone country has been that of a major supplier of the county's drinking water. Being highly porous, and resting on the underlying, impervious Permian marl, it has formed an underground reservoir of vast capacity, providing a high quality water which can be pumped to the surface. The Sherwood Sandstone outcrop terminates rather abruptly in the south at Nottingham, in the form of the majestic Castle Rock, an ancient river cliff of the Trent.

To the east of the rolling sandstone country lie the Keuper rocks with, at their base, the Colwick Formation (Waterstones) forming a low but noticeable escarpment running north from Nottingham to beyond Ollerton. But the most important sediments of the Keuper times are the Mercia Mudstones (Keuper Marls). These are soft, reddish calcareous mudstones and siltstones with occasional hard sandstone or 'skerry' bands.

Despite being of relatively low elevation, the landscape of these Mercia Mudstones, flanking the River Trent, is pleasing and varied. The Keuper rocks are a reminder of the county some 235 million years ago as a hot and arid desert plain, dotted with salt lakes and susceptible to flash floods. It was in and around these evaporating salty lakes that gypsum was formed, and today large-scale excavation of thin, granular layers of gypsum contributes approximately 45% of the UK output. This apparently inhospitable environment was not conducive to life, and consequently few fossils are found except for occasional remains of fish and the preserved footprints of primitive four-limbed animals which wandered by the muddy edges of the desert lakes. It is fortunate that the red, calcareous mudstones of the Keuper marl break down to a fairly heavy and reasonably fertile soil, well suited to mixed farming, in sharp contrast to the poorer and lighter soils of the sandstone country to the west.

The most easterly or perhaps south-easterly of our pattern of north-south bands are the clays and limestones known as the Lias, with the Rhaetic limestones and shales at the base. These deposits resulted from the flooding, about 190 million years ago, of the old desert plain, and its replacement by a shallow sea which covered much of the Midlands. The Rhaetic shales and limestones are marked by a low and often wooded escarpment which can be traced from Somerset through south Nottinghamshire to Lincolnshire. In Nottinghamshire it produces the distinctive Gotham, West Leake and Easte Leake hills. Nestling at the foot of this north-west facing escarpment are the open cast workings and hidden mines which exploit the seams of the gypsum in the upper levels of the underlying Keuper marls. At Red Hill, by the River Soar, the small scale mining of a form of gypsum called alabaster goes back to medieval times. South-eastwards, beyond the Rhaetic escarpment, it is noticeable that the characteristic reddish brown soils derived from the Mercia Mudstone give way to the tenacious grey-olive-brown clay soils of the Lias, in the low-lying Vale of Belvoir. Occasional small ridges in the landscape are the reflection of thin beds of clayey limestones formerly quarried for cement. The Lias clays and limestones were laid down in a shallow sea which was often rich with life. Over the years, many a fossil ammonite or bi-valved shellfish has been picked by inquisitive fingers from ploughed fields. Also, quarrying for limestone in the past at Barnstone, Cropwell Bishop and Staunton has revealed the considerable remains of the swimming reptiles, ichthyosaurus and plesiosaurus.

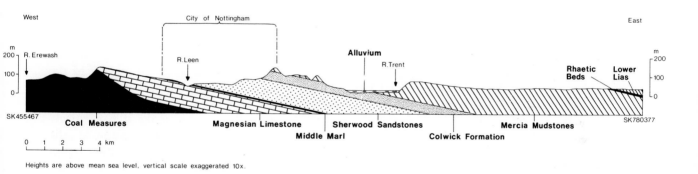

A simplified geological cross section of the county.

About 400 thousand years ago, the climate in the northern hemisphere got progressively colder. Glaciers formed on high ground in this country and moved south. On two separate occasions Nottinghamshire was engulfed by ice, and on a third and last occasion the glacier stopped just short of the county boundary with Yorkshire. The effect of the glaciers was most significant. In the Vale of Belvoir, glaciers advancing from the north probably eroded vast quantities of Lias clay from the northern end of the Vale and deposited them in the south, in the area known as the Nottinghamshire Wolds. All over the county the patterns of rocks outcropping in north-south bands may be confused by sporadic spreads of glacial debris (boulder clay) or by a thin veneer of sands and gravels left by glacial melt waters.

The glaciers, and resulting glacial remains, inevitably affected the drainage pattern and particularly that of the River Trent. Before the Ice Ages the Trent flowed from west to east across the county, taking a course just south of Nottingham, not to the Humber as it does today, but

15

across the Vale of Belvoir and through the Ancaster gap into the Wash. The last glaciation changed its course. Blocked by a lobe of ice or small, stagnant glacier in the Vale of Belvoir, the Trent went northwards at Nottingham to join the Humber. Then the Trent was a much bigger river and, swollen with melt water, it had great erosive power. Today, the imposing and wooded river cliffs at Clifton, Castle Rock, Colwick, Radcliffe and Kneeton bear witness to this mighty river, carving for itself a great trench-like route to the sea. Along its path, the swollen Trent disgorged large quantities of sand and gravel, which have been extracted in modern times to the great benefit of the county's economy, and of its birdlife, which has found the resulting gravel pits a congenial and productive habitat.

In addition to the geology and topography of a county, the other great natural element in its make-up is its climate. Its central position has helped to produce a relatively pleasant one, which tends to avoid extremes of weather found elsewhere. Some idea of the pattern (although there are, of course, local variations due to altitude or other factors) can be gained from figures provided by the Nottingham Weather Centre for 1941-1986. Average daytime temperatures vary from 20.1C in July to 5.3C in January. The wettest month is August with 69.3mm of rain and the driest is March with 52.6mm. The yearly rainfall total averages about 711mm. (The annual average rainfall figure for England and Wales is 912mm.) The general tendency is for rainfall to decrease from west to east, as the county's altitude drops from the Derbyshire border. Living up to its 'flaming' reputation, June is the sunniest month, with 180 hours of sunshine compared to the gloomy days of December which can only muster about 39. In a normal year Nottinghamshire shivers under just over 50 frosts. The combination of soils and climate provides the county's farmers with a growing season of between 240 and 250 days.

While wind and weather may contribute to the shaping of the landscape, and the county's geology tells its own astonishing story of the creation and destruction of deserts, forests and seas, in modern Nottinghamshire it is man who is the greatest shaper and manipulator. Today, despite the variety and richness of wildlife which can be found everywhere in the county, the Nottinghamshire landscape is almost completely man-made. There is a long, if not entirely continuous, history of human settlement, perhaps dating back 70,000 years, according to the findings made in the caves at Creswell Crags. However, it is in the area of the Trent Valley, with its fertile and easily worked soils, that evidence of some of the most important early human settlements has been found. (The many gravel workings in the area do make it particularly suitable for finds of this kind.) Flint hand axes and other material from the Lower and Middle Palaeolithic cultures, for example, have been found at Attenborough and Beeston. (Other traces of later periods have also been discovered along the Trent, such as Bronze Age weapons and metalwork at Attenborough, Clifton, Fiskerton, Holme Pierrepont and Newark.) Again at Creswell, it is clear that Church Hole was used by man between 8750 and 7000 BC. At that stage and for some time afterwards, human activity, based as it was upon hunting and gathering, did not impose any real change on the environment. This had to wait until the first Neolithic farmers, of at least 5,000 years ago, began to make space by felling woodland. From these misty, early times man has continued to leave an indelible impression at every period. The Romans, for example, built one of their great roads—the Fosse Way—through the county, from Willoughby on the Wolds in the south to Brough in the east, bringing people and their civilisation in its wake. (Other notable roads have followed since then, such as the A1 and the M1.) Two fort sites at Thorpe and Margidunum (near Bingham), helped to protect Roman interests. Away from the Fosse, Roman villa sites have been found at Southwell, Mansfield Woodhouse, Barton in Fabis, Cromwell, Epperstone and elsewhere.

Although modern-day Nottinghamshire is one of the smaller English shire counties it has the seventh largest population at just over one million. Much of this is concentrated in the western half, especially in the urban areas of Greater Nottingham and Mansfield-Ashfield. Compared to the national economy, there has been a tradition for a relatively large proportion of male employment in the primary sector, such as agriculture, mining and quarrying. Greater Nottingham has supported a fairly mixed economy including pharmaceuticals, telecommunications, general engineering, textiles and clothing (now somewhat in decline) and bicycle making. Owing to its lowland character, there are no substantial areas too rugged to farm, so most of the available land has been used for this purpose. The process begun by those first tentative farmers has continued with enormous energy and effectiveness. Agricultural land, in fact, makes up about 70% of the county, and much of it is above average quality. Principal crops include wheat, barley, sugar beet, potatoes, oil seed rape, with smaller areas of peas, carrots, sprouts and red beet. Grassland, supporting beef and dairy cattle and sheep, now covers only 20% of the county, with a 20-30% reduction in grassland acreage occurring the last 10-15 years in some areas, such as the Mercia Mudstone country east of the Trent. In contrast to this, the county's crop of oil seed rape has expanded considerably. In 1971, 23 hectares (57 acres) were planted, but by 1984 this had increased to 12,196 hectares (30,000 acres). (This may now have reached a plateau.) Opinions differ widely on the aesthetic appeal of the now commonplace, spectacularly yellow fields of rape, but its place in the local farming economy can hardly be doubted. Horticultural products of the county include top and soft fruit, nursery stock and roses.

This then is the foundation upon which the variety, beauty and fascination of the nature of Nottinghamshire can be explored.

The story opens by returning to a far-distant Nottinghamshire, with the last Ice Age in retreat, the temperatures rising and the people of the county thinking about taking to the land.

Castle Rock, Nottingham. (KM)

ABOVE: Nottinghamshire — spring barley growing in the shadow of Sutton Colliery. (BC) LEFT: A relic of some of Nottinghamshire's very earliest wildlife. A flipper bone from a plesiosaurus found in Staunton Quarry nature reserve. (NTNC) RIGHT: Another crop of potatoes at Cotgrave. (BC)

Woodland — Ancient and Modern

(KM)

About 10,000 years ago the new topography formed by the ice sheets and the melt-waters of their retreat became clothed somewhat thinly with grasses, alpine flowers and bushes of dwarf birch. As the climate improved, trees of Scots pine, juniper, aspen and willow were added. A further 2,000 years of rising temperature and increasing rainfall made it possible for the rest of our familiar plants and animals to travel north, and to settle here before the rising sea level cut us off from the continent. Prolific forests of small-leaved lime, hazel, oak, elm, ash and birch were now established over the Midland regions. Our Mesolithic hunting ancestors were part of the forest fauna. Nottinghamshire alone had about 700 square miles of primeval forest or wildwood.

The wildwood seems to have survived relatively untroubled for another 2,000 years, easily accommodating the Mesolithic hunter-gatherers. However, about 6,000 years ago, Neolithic farmers brought the first significant changes. These early settlers, the squatters of prehistory, would obviously choose a location near water, a river bank or copious spring and from there, with axes of stone, would start to cut the forest back and upwards from their settlements. One can imagine deforestation proceeding from several separate points until there was a meeting of farmers from adjacent areas. No doubt a boundary was agreed and so, on the hillside remote from the settlement, a belt of wildwood was left,but one already changed.Lime was much reduced, for it grew best on the richest soil already cleared, and no doubt further reduced because its soft stringy bark made excellent binding material. Today it is a rarity in Nottinghamshire woods. Elm, too, declined dramatically, for it made good cattle fodder and perhaps experienced a periodic attack of the disease causing its present retreat.

Later Bronze and Iron Age peoples accelerated the felling, using more efficient metal tools. Indeed, probably before Roman times, the forest had been cleared from much of the light sandy soils. Aerial photographs of crop marks taken near Babworth, Retford indicate an extensive, well-defined field system, with regularly spaced boundary ditches covering many miles, suggesting a systematically organised agriculture.

By 1086, when the Domesday Book was compiled, it is thought that the Nottinghamshire countryside looked not unlike our own, with small patches of residual woodland in most parishes, in all perhaps 12% of the county. The Domesday commissioners classed most of the woodland as 'Wood Pasture', indicating that farm animals roamed freely, grazing out a great deal of the ground flora. The conurbations of Nottingham and Mansfield, housing a vastly increased modern population, have of course swallowed extensive tracts of this.

By medieval times, indiscriminate interference by man, and destruction of emerging seedlings by grazing animals, had further impoverished the remains of the wildwood. Some necessary protection was given by a statute in 1483, in the reign of King Edward IV, decreeing the closure of

19

woods for seven years, after cutting 'with sufficient hedges to keep all manner of Beasts and other Cattle out of the same Ground for the preservation of their young Spring', that is, the fresh shoots. In fact wide banks topped with hedges can still be seen in some of our old woods, for example at Gamston Wood.

Broadleaved trees, when cut down, spring to life again quickly; willow can produce three metre (10ft) shoots in a year. The statute ensured that compartments of the woods cut at seven, fourteen or longer intervals were protected from grazing and from people seeking firewood. This rotational cutting, the much discussed coppicing cycle, provided the villagers with a wide variety of materials from slender shoots for baskets to poles for house-building, while regular removal of woody growth exposed the ground to light and helped the survival of the original flora and attendant insects.

Can we identify the remaining shreds of the wildwood and distinguish them from newer plantations? A glance at the Ordnance Survey map of the county will show quite a number of woods bearing a parish or village name. Closer inspection reveals that these are on or very near a parish boundary, where we would expect to find wildwood relics; also, and best observed in spring, we find the flora is richer and more unusual than that of the ash and willow holts and fox coverts of more recent planting. Ancient woods retain assemblages of plants not found in new plantations, and these, once identified, can indicate its antiquity.

Climatic improvement allowed a northerly movement from Europe of the flora and fauna now accepted here as native. Warm periods brought many woodland plants but some, although well established in the early forest, are in the present cooler climate unable to compete with more vigorous species. They are less able to form viable seeds and perhaps need the more stable temperature and moisture control of a woody environment. Vegetative reproduction, where present, is slow. They tend to stay in one place, are quite unable to cross arable land, but many have survived down the centuries in these now isolated patches of woodland. Notable examples are herb paris, a rare and curious four leaved plant with a single flower preferring an undisturbed shady habitat. In folklore, its fruit (a single black berry) was said to be an antidote to witchcraft and the plague but, as it contains an irritant poison, it is debatable whether the disease or the 'cure' was the more harmful.

Wood anemone, the wind flower with its dainty nodding heads, can carpet large areas within a wood but rarely travels far beyond its boundary.

Scented woodruff, called 'new mown hay' in Nottinghamshire, rarely strays more than a few yards from a wood margin.

Wood sorrel, with a preference for damp patches, bears fragile white bells and delicate pale green trefoil leaves, contrasting beautifully with the deep amethyst of bluebells.

Yellow archangel, in Nottinghamshire called bee nettle or yellow deadnettle, is a showy plant with patchy distribution throughout a wood. There are others: dog's mercury, for example, can shade out acres of more delicate plants but, in the arable Midlands, is not common outside old woods. Grasses too, such as wood melick, can be useful pointers. Woody indicators include wild service, small leaved lime, hazel and woodland hawthorn. Several of these species together in one location strongly indicates an ancient source.

Today the best surviving examples of ancient woods in Nottinghamshire are in the northern half, mainly in Bassetlaw on the Mercia Mudstone (Keuper Marl) ridge which runs north and south between the rivers Idle and Trent. More sparsely populated than the southern part, it is gently undulating, a patchwork of hedged fields, small woods and comfortable red pantiled villages. Green lanes are plentiful and particularly in spring the hedgerows are bright, with a wide range of flowers. The mudstone or marl usually weathers to a heavy, reddish, ill-drained clay, clinging tenaciously to boots and farm machinery alike. In spite of this, the soil, when well worked, can be fertile and rewarding. In this countryside, with little natural building stone, the parish woods, which we may conclude are remnants of the wildwood, were cherished down the centuries as a renewable source of timber.

In 1086 nearly every village in this area, once called the 'Clays', had some woodland, in all about 30 woods, and of these about a third remain, most reduced in size but still bearing a parish name. Examples are Beckingham, Wheatley, Kirton, Kneesall, Laxton and Treswell woods, containing much neglected coppice and often with intrusive aliens such as sycamore. Regrettably, Egmanton Wood is covered with well-grown conifers, the only clues to its ancient origin being a few isolated anemone plants and bushes of wild service, while Eaton, Gamston and Wellow woods have been partially coniferised, but still retain an interesting ground flora.

Several other parishes in Bassetlaw have similarly placed woods with assemblages of familiar indicator plants, but bearing names such as Castle Hill Wood in Grove parish, Bluebell Wood in Clarborough, Caddow Wood in North Leverton parish, Headon Park and Beverley Spring Wood in Headon parish. Are these also remnants of village woods, recorded in Domesday?

Little Gringley parish has no woodland except for a patch of scrub in the old gypsum pits, but on its southern boundary is a small stream which still bears on its banks oak and hazel, primroses, bluebells, yellow archangel and anemones. Until recently a 12 hectare (30 acre) wood grew here, bounded on one side by this stream but, in the early 1960s, it was converted to agriculture. On the north side of Retford Gate, possibly a Roman trackway through North Leverton to the Trent crossing at Littleborough, is an ancient hedge with little thorn in it, but made of maple, oak, hazel, dogwood and honeysuckle, beneath which grow dog's mercury, primrose, wood anemone with stitchwort, campion and bugle. Cowslips and violets spatter the foreground. Reference to Chapman's Nottinghamshire Map of 1774 shows that the nearby Caddow Wood grew right up to this lane, where an arable field now lies. This hedge was not planted, but almost certainly derived from the margin of the old wood, still a fairyland of indicator flowers. These habitats are valuable, for not only are they a delight to look at, but they provide evidence of an earlier landscape.

However, down the centuries and particularly in the last 40 years there has been sporadic but continuous erosion of these historically significant woodlands with their valuable biological remnants. Present-day destruction, whether by conversion to barley fields or to conifer plantations, is irreversible, for the latter, by blanketing out light and acidifying the ground, eliminates all but the hardiest of plants. The indicators with but a tenuous hold on their habitat are the first to succumb. No replanting scheme, however imaginatively designed, can reproduce the richness and variability of a fragment of wildwood.

Indeed, concern about the threats to our remaining old woods has been a major element in the development of the county's nature conservation movement.

Fortunately some ancient woods have already been acquired as nature reserves. Treswell Wood, for example, differs from most old woods in that it has lost little of its original area. In 1086 it had the equivalent of about 58 hectares (144 acres) but by the middle of the 18th century 13 hectares (32 acres) had been assarted (converted to agriculture). Its structure is that of coppice with standards, in which trees of ash and oak are normally allowed to grow on to large timber, while the underwood of hazel, maple, thorn and sallow is coppiced at regular intervals. In the 18th and early 19th century, when villagers made their own ale, documentary evidence shows that ash was regularly coppiced at Treswell. In the wood's record book of 1824 we find:

'To 7820 stakes at 3s per hundred	£11 14s 6d
To 9080 bindings at 3s per hundred	£13 12s 6d
To 710 round poles at 6d each	£17 15s 0d
2760 hop poles at 30s per hundred	£41 08s 0d'
Felled oak was stripped of bark for the tanning industry	
'14 tons 12cwts of oak bark at 21s per ton	£15 06s 7d
Paid to the barkers for ale	£ 0 07s 6d'

Many indicator plants are still present, together with a variety of woodland orchids such as the waxy white butterfly orchid, patches of early purple orchid and a scattering of the broad-leaved helleborine, showing that centuries of regular cutting and clearing has not destroyed, but almost certainly encouraged, the ground flora. A year after coppicing there is an increase of ground flora diversity, and this surge of bloom continues for two or three years until the growing coppice once more shades it out. After years of neglect this traditional form of management was reintroduced in 1974. Over 10 years of ride clearance and coppicing has clearly enriched the ground flora, provided extensive stretches of herbage for insects, and a succession of habitats for birds and small mammals.

Insects abound. A repellent cream is advisable on a warm August day at Treswell. Over 50 species of brightly coloured hoverfly have been recorded, some imitating wasps, and most poised like hummingbirds above a leaf looking for mates. Many flightless insects such as the speckled bush-cricket, rare in the Midlands, still live here, another indicator of the great age of the wood, for they too are unable to cross arable land.

The well-cleared rides and occasional glades have been undeniably beneficial to moths and butterflies. Of 45 species of moth caught in one survey, five of these were rarities in the county—blotched emerald, normally a southern species, small white wave and lilac beauty, both very local; twin spot carpet, a northern species, and gold swift, one of the few sightings of this moth in the county.

Those mothlike small butterflies, the large and small skippers, are frequent inhabitants. A hopeful sight on a warm February day is the bright yellow of the male brimstone butterfly, followed later in spring by orange tips, small whites and greenveined whites, easily distinguished from the former by the heavily shadowed veins on the underside of the wings. The vivid tortoiseshells, peacocks and red admirals, and occasionally a painted lady, parade the rides. Each year more commas, bright orange with frilly wings, are reported. Meadow browns, gatekeepers and walls are the most noticeable browns, while ringlets, once scarce, are on the increase. Small coppers, and common blues, which love open grassy places are here, and purple hairstreak has been seen.

Thorough surveys of other invertebrates have not yet been undertaken in our northern woods, certainly when compared to the detailed observations in Sherwood Forest, but nestboxes in Treswell Wood are an interesting source of information. As there are no large old trees there to provide nesting holes for birds, a variety of boxes has been erected. The discarded nesting material is regularly examined. Dead fledglings attract the orange and black sexton beetle, while a predator of insect larvae is *Gnathoncus buyssoni*, too rare to merit a common name. A record of this species at Treswell was a first for Nottinghamshire and the Midlands. Earwigs and woodlice are common, and bird fleas occur in abundance, the latter strategically positioned around the entrance holes, awaiting visiting birds.

A lover of sheltered damp places is the tree slug, a greyish sometimes translucent slug of 7—8cm. It climbs readily into next boxes and is rare in the dry Midlands — probably another stay-at-home, indicating the wood's great age.

Wasps and bumble bees invade boxes as they would holes in old trees. A tit box invaded by wasps, abandoned by its owners, was later the home or a successful brood of wrens, which had incorporated the wasp nesting material into their own.

A regular, systematic, bird-ringing scheme over the last ten years has revealed much detailed information on bird movement and nesting preferences. Birds do not seem unduly troubled by the coppice rotation. Grasshopper warblers will move into a newly cleared coppice compartment, but blackcaps will choose an older site with invasive bramble.

The population of about three dozen species of permanent residents, such as finches and tits, wrens and robins, stockdoves, wood pigeons, woodcocks and pheasants, can at times be doubled by regular migrants such as fieldfare and redwing, brambling, bunting and goldcrests in the winter, and in summer by the breeding blackcaps, willow and garden warblers. Clearing undergrowth has made easier hunting territory for tawny owls and sparrowhawks. Occasional visitors are mallard, teal, kingfisher, barn and little owl and green woodpecker. Great and lesser spotted woodpeckers and nuthatches breed successfully, the latter preferring old woodpeckers' nest-holes to the special boxes hung for them. Tawny owls regularly use nest boxes, rearing one or two youngsters and providing, through pellets and the remains of prey items, a list of their victims. Commonly found are blue and great tits, blackbirds, thrushes, starlings, tree sparrows and wood pigeons. Many of these were ringed birds. The expected small mammals were there, the diet topped up with moles and rabbits and recently, in revenge for predation of its eggs, the hind paw of a grey squirrel.

Of the small hole boxes erected for tits, about half are occupied by the target species. Special woodpecker boxes stuffed with polystyrene are ignored by those birds but sought after by coal tits for roosting, while one enterprising blue tit excavated a roomy nesting cavity and successfully reared a brood in this well-insulated home. Great tits demonstrate a wide range of nest design. Given the same box depth, some have the barest of covering, while others pile up to 30 centimetres of moss on top of the basal twigs.

In general, blue and great tits are the most reliable customers, and wrens are becoming more confident of the boxes, especially the open, narrow-slit box.

As Britain was once predominantly woodland, it follows that most of our familiar native animals prefer its sheltered and moderated climate. Moles are still active in the wood when the pastures outside are fast frozen. There have been no resident badgers in the last few years, but the stream banks in the surrounding cultivated land do have them, often the proud boast of a local farmer. Weasels, and stoats, occasionally seen in ermine, rival the grey squirrels in predation of nest boxes. A steep-sided ditch provides home and playground for the dark-backed water shrews, once seen repeatedly climbing up the muddy bank, to glissade down again with a plop into the water.

This wood is untroubled by deer damage but is visited occasionally by passing roe deer.

About four miles westward of Treswell and adjacent to each other are the woods of Eaton and Gamston parishes, respectively 24 and 40 hectares (60 and 100 acres) which, like Treswell Wood, are nature reserves. They run along the scarp above the River Idle and, on a bright clear evening, the sunset views across the valley are magnificent, often extending to the Derbyshire hills.

Some years ago both woods came under the control of the Forestry Commission, which clear-felled and planted conifers over much of the area. The native scrub struck back so vigorously that many of the conifers were dwarfed or smothered, and the rich ground flora survived.

The history of the two woods diverged about 1,000 years ago. Eaton Wood, in the 11th century the larger, bears patches of ridge and furrow, showing that at one time, perhaps before the Black Death, it was partially felled and cultivated. The occurrence of herb paris and other slow, shy colonisers throughout implies that it must have reverted to woodland many centuries ago. Gamston Wood has its large medieval boundary banks, and its interior holds several wet depressions, which often characterise woods of ancient origin. Together, these two woods, with their overspill of rare plants onto the roadside verges, offer some of the richest and most colourful assemblages of plants in the county.

On the Eaton side, ditching has revealed flint cores and arrowheads, which carry us back to the camp of a Mesolithic family, contriving their tools and perhaps watching the valley below for signs of game. The discovery of a broken Neolithic axe head speaks perhaps of a frustrated early farmer trying to tame the wildwood.

Arrowheads and orchids, bark for tanning and the hoot of a tawny owl, hop poles and butterflies are all part of the fascinating past and present of these ancient Nottinghamshire woods. However, elsewhere in the county another woodland story can be told.

The true woodlands or coppice-woods discussed so far were already, by the time of Domesday, fairly isolated features on the fertile lowland soils of England, such as in North and East Nottinghamshire; by then, it is estimated, around 80% of the natural forest of England had been cleared by man's activities. But to the north-west of the Trent lies a great tract of infertile sandland, which had not been much cleared of its trees or populated by men by the time of the Norman Conquest, simply because of its unsuitability for agriculture. The wood that remained here and dominated the county of Nottingham (for that reason known as 'Shire Wood' later Sherwood) was a natural choice for a Norman Royal Forest, both for its size and its strategic position, looking north against the unfriendly Scottish tribes.

It is important, in trying to understand the forces which shaped a Royal Forest, to realise that Royal Forests were not simply pleasure grounds for idle tyrants, or indeed that Royal Forests were necessarily covered with dense woods all belonging to the King. At Sherwood as elsewhere they were chosen for their potential as hunting areas and provisioning centres for a ruling class, which governed and defended its territory not from a central seat (as at London), but on the move. The larger Royal Forests (such as Sherwood) contained towns and hamlets with adjoining arable land, pasture, orchards, fisheries, osier beds, even private farms and woods. Indeed, most of the land was privately or commonly held, the King having only the right to deer and (usually) timber, except on his own demesne, that is his own freehold land. Therefore Royal Forest was not so much the King's Woods as a legal or taxation area administered by a particular set of bye-laws, and within which certain activities were subject to constraint. As such, it can be compared with our modern National Parks (although the penalties for breaking bye-laws have grown less severe over the centuries!). Moreover, with the passage of time, the establishment of Commoner's rights became as powerful an influence as those of the Crown in the preservation of Royal Forests. Thus the development of the habitat inside the old Royal Forest boundary falls into place. It is the story of a landscape both preserved and destroyed by law.

On the one hand Forest Law caused the preservation of great oaks way beyond their life-span in a normally managed wood; on the other, while the attention paid by the King's officers to the re-establishment of young trees appears to have been only intermittent, stock-grazing, which was the main activity permitted to the local population as a livelihood, gained in importance. The history of Sherwood was a gradual progression (or rather deterioration) through a series of habitats—the three 'W's: true Woodland, then Wood Pasture, then forest Waste. After nearly 1,000 years of this process, there remains none of the first, a little of the second, and somewhat more of the third. Any true woodland, with undergrowth and a varied ground flora, had been grazed away from Sherwood centuries ago by generations of deer and forest breeds of sheep, pigs and cattle. In this respect, the Domesday Book woods and their flora have survived in a much more intact way.

Wood pasture is found only on Parks, Chases and Royal Forests. Right up to the 17th century, a great part of Sherwood was still Wood Pasture. However, a massive amount of felling without replacement occurred in the Civil War.By the end of the 18th century (by which time the Crown was disentangling and organising the final sale of its Forest rights to the large landowners in the Dukeries), there was already more Waste than Wood Pasture. Fortunately the then Duke of Portland at Welbeck and second Earl of Manvers at Thoresby appreciated the historical and aesthetic value of the remaining areas and, by preserving them, perhaps qualify as our first-ever conservationists. In her diary in 1844 Queen Victoria described the ancient woodlands in terms still relevant today: 'Though they have been long cleared of underwood, they still contain many large and venerable oaks in every stage of perfection and decay'. In addition to the unique wildlife value of these trees, it is unlikely that any other habitat in Britain is capable of such surrealistic moods.

To any natural historian whose ecological experience has been developed in true woodland, the first noticeable aspect of ancient Wood Pasture is probably what is missing. The tree species are limited (principally by former browsing from large herbivores), largely to oak and birch. It is likely that hazel and small-leaved lime were constituents of the original woodland, but neither are present now. (Today, with grazing no longer a significant factor, rowan and holly are re-asserting themselves.) Ground vegetation is even more impoverished (again as a result of having been grazed out): bracken is the predominant ground species, with very little variation indeed. It is interesting to note the complaint of the famous Nottinghamshire historian, Thoroton, writing in 1677, that 'there will not very shortly be Wood enough left to cover the Bilberies, which every summer were wont to be an extraordinary great profit and pleasure to poor people'. Bilberry is only found in one or two small patches in the whole of the old Sherwood area. It would, in short, be hard to make the usual deductions about the original habitat type from so impoverished a flora. Yet in some remarkable respects, Wood Pasture retains features of the former wildwood far more faithfully than any other primary woodland type. These include many of the life forms which are associated with the ancient trees of Sherwood and, in particular, its extraordinary variety of invertebrates. Woodland flowers may be vivid reminders of the age of some woods, but the invertebrates of Sherwood can also speak eloquently of the antiquity of the place.

Forest Waste was merely the logical product of Wood Pasture from which the trees had been removed. On the poor, acid soil of Sherwood, this produces a form of heathland, though the exact nature of heathland in Sherwood may be fairly complex. For example, consider the implications of the following statement from the Crown Commissioner's Report of 1793: 'The Towns and Villages in the Forest have a Privilege which is called inclosing Brecks: This is a Power to inclose, and plough, a certain quantity, generally about 300 Acres, of the Waste of the Forest, to keep it in Tillage for Seven Years, and to inclose and cultivate a similar Quantity, on prostrating the Fences, and laying open the former'. There is a clear possibility that in places the heathland of Forest Waste has seen cultivation. What is certain is that huge tracts of Waste, whether heathland or reverted scrub, still existed in the early years of this century on the old Rufford estate, but were planted up by the Forestry Commission in the 1930s. Interestingly enough, in one or two areas which have been cleared of conifers by wind-blow and never re-planted (such as the site being presently developed as a nature reserve on a holiday development area in Pittance Park), a heathland ecology appears to be strongly re-asserting itself. Even during the few years following a forestry clear-fell, certain important heathland species such as the nightjar take advantage of the temporary heathland-like conditions.

Further north, in the Budby area, heathland may be found on the Army Training Areas, although it has suffered until recently a large amount of birch encroachment, because of the absence of grazing. The birch scrub has now been almost completely cleared, the aim being to preserve lowland heath characteristics. Heathland species of interest include a peculiar, glaucous variety of ling and occasional patches of petty whin. Ornithological interest has declined in recent times. The woodlark is no longer recorded. However, the birch clearance may be beneficial to birds. In a few year's time it may be possible to see the woodlark again and perhaps be pleasantly surprised by the occasional stonechat. The heathland is also home to some of Sherwood's many legions of moths.

Today the only surviving area of ancient woodland which once formed part of the Royal Forest is known as Birklands. Approximately 185 hectares (460 acres) of land, containing oaks approaching 500—600 years, are now managed as a Country Park by Nottinghamshire County Council. This area has also been designated a Site of Special Scientific Interest by the Nature Conservancy Council, primarily as an ancient, oak woodland habitat, but more specifically because of the important populations of invertebrates it supports.

The past management of the woodland has resulted in four distinct age groups within the oak population. The most recent are the young trees, which have grown up over the last 30—40 years. Although rabbits have controlled natural regeneration during this period, the outbreak of myxomatosis during the 1950s did allow many oak seedlings to develop, free from the predations of rabbits on their spring growth.

The next two groups contain trees of 60—120 years old and 150—250 years old respectively. The former developed when the rights of pannage (pigs grazing on acorns) ceased, the latter being trees which were only seedlings when management effectively stopped. This leaves approximately 1,000 ancient oaks (300—500 years old) — perhaps Queen Victoria's 'large and venerable oaks' — still surviving in the forest today. It is these trees and the dead wood that falls from them which provide the area with such an outstanding wealth of invertebrate life.

The spider population of Birklands and the associated heathland of Budby South Forest totals over one third of all British species. The site has been described as amongst the top ten in Britain, having a wide variety of species and containing some which are indeed rare. Considering the almost complete lack of water in the area, this remarkable diversity of spiders is even more noteworthy.

Why then should this area of ancient woodland and heath be so notable for its population of, not only spiders, but also other invertebrate groups? The answer probably lies in the historical development of the area. There has been no radical change in land use during its vegetational development. Therefore, invertebrate species, after their colonisation, have had ample opportunity to establish viable populations over a long period. The often drastic habitat changes found elsewhere, caused by alterations in land use, have had little impact here. Indeed, Nottinghamshire should consider itself fortunate in having Sherwood within its boundaries. There are few other ancient woodland sites of such distinction left in the British Isles.

In addition, the oak has long been regarded as an important host to invertebrate life and it is the presence of such an age range of trees which has enabled the insect and spider populations to become so large.

The old trees support such rare spiders as *Lepthyphantes midas*, a small, inconspicuous 'money spider' recorded from the area at the turn of the century, but thought to have disappeared until its re-discovery the late 1970s. Many of these creatures are only known by their scientific name, (generally derived from the Latin or Greek) which nonetheless often gives a lucid description of some aspect of the species. For example, *Lepthyphantes* derives from the Greek 'leptes' meaning thin and 'hyphantes' meaning a web. English names, when used, are also descriptive, but the advantage of scientific names is that they are universal. English names can cause confusion — the English harebell is called a bluebell in Scotland.

Tuberta macrophthalma, another nationally rare spider, is fairly common within the old oaks, leaving its tell-tale, papery egg-sac dotted around within hollow trees and in the cracks of dead timber. Both *Tuberta macrophthalma* and *Lepthyphantes midas* are small (2—3mm) and dark coloured, and depend upon an undisturbed woodland habitat, having had trees or woodland present for a long period. A more impressive spider, competing to rank as one of Britain's largest is *Meta bourneti*. Its body length reaches about 20mm (¾") but it is the long, glossy, brown legs which increase its size to a fearsome 50mm (2") total length. Until fairly recently it was regarded as a cave-dwelling species, preferring dark, damp conditions not only naturally, but also in drains and sewers. However, it has turned up at Sherwood (only males have been recorded so far).In the absence of a web it possibly finds large spaces within old hollow oak trees are suitable sites to spin its large orb-web.

Other more colourful species such as *Araniella cucurbitina* and *Araneus marmoreus* are regularly found in the foliage of oaks. The latter spider, again, is somewhat unusual in its preference for Sherwood, being generally regarded as an inhabitant of marsh and bog land. However, its bright, yellow abdomen with a distinctive brown wedge marking can be easily recognised in Birklands during the late summer and early autumn. Spiders abound in the woodland throughout the year, but perhaps the best times are the late spring/early summer and autumn. During May and June, the warmer weather encourages wolf spiders and jumping spiders into activity, making the forest floor come alive with their rapid movement amongst the oak leaf litter. Female wolf spiders are noticeable, carrying their egg-sacs around attached to their spinners. Later on, the female's abdomen seems much larger until one realises that she is carrying a whole bunch of tiny spiderlings around with her. These newly hatched youngsters hitch a ride on their mother's back for two or three days, then disperse to make their own way in the world.

Autumn is the season for orb-webs of different size and variety. Perhaps the best time to appreciate the intricacy of these webs is early on autumn mornings, when the dew or frost picks out each individual strand of silk, highlighting the complex construction of these snares. Sherwood is the home for many brightly-coloured and patterned orb-web spinners.

Cyclosa conica, with its oddly humped abdomen, spins an orb-web with a band of silk, the stabilimentum, woven into it running vertically above and below the hub. The spider sits hunched up in the hub of the web, effectively joining the upper and lower bands of silk, giving an overall impression of a twig caught in the web. It is possible that the stabilimentum (which often includes remnants of past meals) provides a background against which the spider camouflages itself.

The large, nocturnal *Nuctenea umbratica* spins its large orb-web close to a narrow crack in a tree trunk or a fence post, where it lies waiting for some tell-tale disturbance of its web by its potential supper. Its noticeably flattened abdomen enables it to squeeze into the tightest corner, but it can extricate itself remarkably quickly when the need arises.

The areas of ancient *Deschampsia* grassland within the remaining forest area provide ideal habitats for those spiders requiring drier conditions. One family, the crab spiders (*Thomisidae*), includes slow-moving species which creep stealthily around beneath the tussocks of wavy hair grass, preying on the small invertebrates commonly found there. *Xysticus erraticus* and *Xysticus cristatus* are both species regularly recorded, the males going to extraordinary lengths to protect themselves when courting and mating. As a first move, they spin threads over the female to 'tie her down' and prevent her from delivering a potentially poisonous bite, before they approach closer to complete the mating procedure.

Other grassland species recorded from Sherwood include *Tibellus oblongus*, a thin, straw-coloured spider, which camouflages itself to great effect against the grass stems in late summer. *Zora silvestris* also, although a rare species nationally, is present amongst these old grassland areas.

The old trees of the woodland also support small populations of a rare relative, the false scorpion or pseudoscorpion. The rarest member of this group, *Dendrochernes cyrneus*, which occurs at Sherwood is also Britain's largest with a length of 6mm. These tiny creatures resemble their close relatives, the scorpions, in many ways, but lack the fearsome 'sting in the tail'; they do not possess any tail-like appendage. However, they do use poison to paralyse their prey, and it is injected through pincer-like palps (sense organs) when the prey is bitten. *Dendrochernes cyrneus* seems to prefer the conditions found underneath fairly close-fitting bark, on the dead or dying branches and trunks of ancient trees. Oak, however, does not seem to be the only species of tree it inhabits. However, old trees do seem necessary, and long-living oaks are obviously a prime choice.

The information on the beetle fauna of Birklands is patchy although nearly 1,500 species are thought to be present.

Obviously, the existence of so much dead and dying oak timber is of prime importance, both as a shelter to many species and as a source of food to the larvae of many wood-boring beetles. The longhorn beetles are well represented and include the striking wasp beetle which not only resembles a wasp in colour, but more particularly in its erratic movement over the trunks of trees, and in its wasp-like tapping of its antennae. Other longhorns include *Strangalia* species and the much rarer *Saperda scalaris*, a beautiful black and yellowish-green beetle, recorded recently on fallen oak branches. Both recently-fallen wood and that which has lain on the ground a long time form important habitats — each kind for different groups. Loose bark, dry wood and well decomposed fragments form the commoner habitat. The more recently detached branches, however, more closely resemble the parent tree, being damper and having closer-fitting bark and, although found less often, do form an important site for some of the rarer beetles.

The longhorn beetles are not too difficult to discover for many can be found feeding on thistles in late summer. The majority of beetles, however, are unlikely to be encountered without a great deal of patience. Many species inhabit dead or dying timber, their larvae feeding underneath the bark or tunnelling further into the wood itself. As well as the oak, birch trees are an important habitat. The rare click beetles *Ampedus pomona* and *Ampedus pomorum* seem confined to areas of birch. The presence of much rotting birch timber on the ground is important. Although the actual wood is not old (probably fallen from trees less than 50 years old) the existence of so many rare and interesting beetles dependent on it suggests that birch woodland has been present for many hundreds of years. Indeed, the name Birklands derives from the Old Scandinavian 'Birkilundr', meaning birch wood, indicating the possibility of extensive areas of birch as far back as the Viking invasions. The rotting birch wood provides a home for a curious beetle. *Hylecoetus dermestoides*, the males of which have extraordinary fan-like maxillary palps, which are probably used in the courting procedure, as well as in the tasting and selection of food. Another rarity, *Plegaderus dissectus*, is dependent on this rotting birch wood, not because it actually eats it but because the larvae of bark beetles form its main food. Of the carabid group of beetles the rare *Pterostichus oblongopunctatus* is also associated with areas of decaying birch wood.

The bracket fungi of both oak and birch form an important food source for some rare beetles. On oak *Laetiporus sulphureus* and the beefsteak fungus *Fistulina hepatica* are consumed by small black beetles, *Aplocnemus nigricornis* being an unusual example. On birch, *Piptoporus betulinus* starts life as a small, white rounded knob growing from the bark, before developing into the large, flat bracket fungus commonly seen in birch woodland. This fungus supplies a food source for a whole host of beetles, many of them small, shiny and predominantly black creatures which tunnel into its depths. The pretty *Triplax russica* is a common example, although it has bright orange legs and thorax, contrasting with its shiny, black wing cases.

Other beetles found in Sherwood are not specifically dependent on oak or birch, although these trees do provide the right kind of habitat conditions. On the foliage of all types of vegetation many different species of ladybird can be found. The common seven spot ladybird and its varieties are universal. On some of the Scots pine scattered throughout the ancient woodland the large eyed ladybird is regularly recorded. In the oak particularly, and on some hawthorn trees, species such as the twenty-two spot ladybird (black spots on a yellow background) and the cream spot ladybird (cream spots on a brown background) are present.

Others from Sherwood include the green tiger beetle, particularly on open, sandy ground in sunny weather, the common cockchafer or May bug, often seen blundering about with its heavy flight on warm May evenings, and *Lampyris noctiluca*. The female *Lampyris* is more commonly known as the glow-worm, for it is she who on summer evenings attracts males by emitting a strong, greenish light from the tip of her abdomen. The males respond by emitting a series of flashes as they fly around looking for and answering the female's invitation. Although not normally associated with dry acid soils and the vegetation it supports, which is typical of Sherwood, this beetle has been found on the margins of the woodland area. Here, the Forestry Commission's pine plantations shade the woodland ridges, providing the dampish conditions favoured by the small snails which form the basis of the glow-worm's diet.

The large and varied beetle population of Sherwood is there because of the large amount of dead and dying timber, but also the site's geographical location is important. The woodland provides southern species with their most northerly outpost, and conversely many northern species are at their southern limit in Sherwood. In fact, the site is regarded as among the top three in the country as a whole — there is probably nowhere else in Britain where the same species are found in such close proximity. By any standards, it is one of the great and most distinctive glories of the nature of Nottinghamshire.

On the other hand, as is the case with many woodland areas throughout the country, Sherwood has lost many of its butterflies and moths in recent years. The use of agricultural pesticides has probably caused the disappearance of many of the once much commoner species recorded at the turn of the century. However, Sherwood can still boast a few specialities. The angle striped sallow moth, for example, is locally common in the area, its only other important location being South Yorkshire. Its larvae feed on two species of birch — the common silver or warty birch and the downy birch which grow together at Sherwood. The woodland also supports other rare moths. The great oak beauty was described by J.W. Carr as rare in Sherwood, one specimen recorded around the turn of the century. Since then it was thought to have disappeared until its appearance at mercury vapour light traps in the recent past. This is probably an indication of its gradual northern movement through the country. It has excellent camouflage and virtually disappears on landing on the bark of an oak tree. Another uncommon species occasionally seen in flight during the day is the large red underwing. This moth also blends in well with its background as it lies on the bark of the oak. In addition to this defence, if disturbed it lifts its forewings, exposing bright red hindwings, thus confusing a hungry bird for a split-second and enabling the moth to fly away unharmed.

On a warm July evening over a hundred species of moth can be attracted to special mercury vapour lights set up in the woodland. On such an evening they are surrounded by clouds of moths — one could continue counting new species until well into the early hours, for different species fly at different times. A typical list may include the large elephant hawk moth (its larvae feed on rosebay willowherb, a common flowering plant in the woods), the buff-tip, large emerald, lilac beauty, buff arches, map-winged swift, drinker and scarce silver-lines. Many of Sherwood's moths have larvae which are either oak or birch feeders but one cannot discount the lowland heath of Budby South Forest adjacent to Birklands. Here, species such as the grass wave, clouded buff, archer's dart and the Portland moth still survive.

Natterer's bats such as this one are probably part of the mammal population of Sherwood Forest. (WE)

With moths abundant on warm summer evenings it follows that bats, their main predators, will be in evidence. Noctule bats, particularly, find the cracks and hollows of old trees ideal summer roost sites, and can even be heard during the day, chattering and squeaking inside their nursery roosts. At dusk, their high flight betrays their presence, while the fluttering and weaving flight of the pipistrelle occurs at a lower level. Long-eared bats have also been recorded and species such as Natterer's are likely to be present, given the preponderance of the once common bat roost site, the old hollow tree.

Butterflies have probably fared less well than moths over recent years. Species such as the purple emperor recorded by Carr as 'taken at Cossus (goat moth) borings in old oaks in the Forest close to Edwinstowe 13.7.1874', are no longer present and the value of oak woodland for its butterfly population is not really justified in Sherwood's case. The hollow trees provide important over-wintering sites for species like the small tortoiseshell, peacock and brimstone, but, apart from the purple hairstreak, Sherwood cannot boast any other specialities. However, over recent years, the comma butterfly has re-emerged—another southern species gradually extending its northern limits. One can hope, perhaps, for a sight of the speckled wood, a truly woodland butterfly, flitting through the forest glades of Sherwood in the not too distant future.

Many other insects abound in Sherwood but much information has yet to be gathered. However, the hornet appears to be establishing itself building nests in the hollow trunks of trees. Other wasps and bees are well represented in Sherwood, but it is only recently that hornets have been seen. Again, it appears that this species is gradually extending its northern range. Possibly the warm summers of the late 1970s prompted this northern movement. Records throughout the Midlands suggest the phenomenon is not purely local.

With such a rich population of invertebrates of all kinds Sherwood has a natural attraction for those birds which feed on insects. When the vast range of suitable nesting sites in the hollow oak trees is taken into account it is not surprising that the summer bird population of Sherwood numbers about 80 different species. Redstarts are perhaps the most striking summer visitors with the handsome males singing their bubbling song from the highest positions on some of the standing oaks. At least 40 males have been heard singing on a dawn chorus walk at the end of May. Other summer migrants include the wood warbler, blackcap, whitethroat and garden warbler as well as a good number of cuckoos. Of the resident birds the woodpeckers are all represented in Birklands. The great spotted woodpecker is perhaps the most common, taking advantage of the large number of rotting (and therefore fairly soft) birch trunks in which it drills its nest hole. Yet the green woodpecker is not uncommon. An added attraction is the open grassland containing the nests of meadow ants which the 'yaffle' (to give it its country name) loves to raid with its long, sticky tongue. The lesser spotted woodpecker is scarce, but does seem to be strengthening its numbers in the woodland, pairs being recorded during the breeding season in recent years.

Other birds visible throughout the year include the nuthatch and tree creeper. Both are often found together on the trunk of a mature oak tree, competing for the insects sheltering in the deep cracks of the bark. There is a reason. The tree creeper is a methodical feeder. Starting at the base of a tree trunk, the bird will move up and round it on a spiral path, probing the cracks in the bark with its thin, curved beak as it searches for insects. The nuthatch, on the other hand — being virtually the only British bird which can sit upside-down on a tree trunk without falling off — often moves down the tree picking up insects the tree creeper has missed on the way up!

In addition to taking insects the nuthatch, as its name suggests, feeds on a variety of nuts — acorns being the most common within Sherwood. Other birds also depend on acorns for their survival during the cold winter months. Both jays and wood pigeons are active as autumn turns to winter. Hundreds of acorns are taken both as immediate food to build up their fat reserves, and also to bury in small caches around the woodland floor as a readily accessible food supply during the winter period. Some of these acorn stores are forgotten and, with any luck, oak seedlings may develop the following year. The jay and the wood pigeon depend upon the oak for food and the oak relies upon these birds to disperse its seed throughout the woodland.

Large flocks of redpolls are regularly seen during the autumn, moving through areas of silver birch, feeding on birch seed as they go. If winter proves to be severe, redwings and fieldfares often appear in large numbers. Bramblings too are forced this far south by prolonged cold spells in their normal wintering areas.

It may be thought that an area of woodland such as Birklands would, with its large population of small mammals such as wood mice, voles and shrews, attract a wide variety of predatory birds. In fact only tawny owls and kestrels are present in any number. Sparrowhawks and long-eared owls have been recorded, but remain on the edge of the deciduous woodland, where it meets the coniferous plantations of the Forestry Commission.

The tit family is well represented, as is the finch family, although the hawfinch has not been recorded for some time. So, although Sherwood has no real rarities in the bird world, it does provide a marvellous example of woodland habitat, ideal for a large variety of birds.

Other woods in other parts of the county contribute substantially to its landscape and wildlife. These include Seller's Wood in the City of Nottingham, Foxcovert Plantation, Wilford Hill Wood and others. In the south of the county, at the nature reserve at Bunny Old Wood, the western half was donated to the Nottinghamshire Trust for Nature Conservation by British Gypsum in 1985 and, despite the impact of Dutch elm disease, it shares much of the history and fascination of its arguably better known sisters to the north.

Woods have earned a special place in the heart of every lover of the countryside: for their flowers in spring, for the glorious din of the dawn chorus, or for the peace and tranquillity of their snowy rides in winter. Their present state represents just the latest phase of their relationship with a busy and bustling humanity, which has used and abused them in turn. It is to be hoped that today's last vestiges of the wildwood of long ago will now be allowed safety and security, as a home for abundant communities of plants and animals, and as a source of joy to grateful humans.

Some of the ancient oaks of Sherwood. (KM)

LEFT: Wood sorrel prefers damp areas in the woodland. (MB) RIGHT: Herb paris — a typical indicator of ancient woodland. (RHH) BELOW: Leaves of the wild service tree, another indicator plant. (M&DG)

ABOVE: Ancient stag-headed oaks and silver birch in Sherwood Forest. (M&DG) LEFT: The beautiful butterfly orchid is found in Treswell Wood. (M&DG) CENTRE: *Saperda scalaris*, one of the long-horned beetles, is a rare and beautiful insect found recently in Sherwood. (SW/NNHM) BELOW: *Meta bourneti*, found among the ancient oaks of Sherwood, ranks as one of Britain's largest spiders. (JC)

PLATE I

LEFT: The colourful elephant hawkmoth is attracted to mercury vapour lights set up in woodland. (DS)
RIGHT: Male redstarts are some of the most striking summer visitors to Sherwood. (DS) BELOW: Autumn
comes to Sherwood. (M&DG)

PLATE II

ABOVE: Primroses at Eaton Wood. (MB) BELOW: Woodland relic hedge at Retford Gate, Caddow Wood in background. (MB)

ABOVE: Early purple orchid. (MB) RIGHT: Early spring in Treswell —
ash standards. (MB) BELOW: Common blues mating. (DSm)

ABOVE: Stock dove. (JF) BELOW: Tawny owl adult with hungry
youngster. (DS)

LEFT: Tawny owl at roost. (M&DG) RIGHT: The little owl is an
occasional visitor to Treswell Wood. (DS) BELOW: Violets. (RHH)

LEFT: Grey squirrels — woodland residents which provoke very mixed feelings. (DSm) RIGHT: Badgers are popular but elusive creatures. (DW) BELOW: Old boundary bank on the west side of Gamston Wood. (MB)

ABOVE: Woodland hawthorn in blossom. (MB) BELOW: A ride in Eaton
Wood, early May. (MB)

38

ABOVE: Recent management at Eaton Wood — cleared area under ash.
(MB) BELOW: Bracket fungi found on trees in Sherwood: LEFT: *Laetiporus
sulphureus;* (BVC) RIGHT: *Piptoporus betulinus.* (BVC)

LEFT: A birchwood ride in Sherwood. (M&DG) RIGHT: Elephant hawkmoth caterpillar. (AL)

ABOVE: Wood warblers are summer visitors to Sherwood (notice the leg ring). (DS) BELOW: A ravenous baby cuckoo dwarfs its dunnock 'parent'. (DS)

LEFT: A long-eared owl, a scarce visitor to Sherwood, feeds its young. (DS)
RIGHT: The nightjar is an exciting heath-land bird of the county. (JF)
BELOW: Petty whin (near Edwinstowe). (M&DG)

Eaton (north) and Gamston Woods (south) from the air. (NCC)

ABOVE: Fallow deer. (DSm) BELOW: Red deer, always alert and on the
lookout. (SM)

44

The Dukeries

(KM)

It may at first sight seem extremely curious, in a book dividing the county into habitats, to see the name of an area in northish Nottinghamshire where an unusually large concentration of landed estates and stately homes once existed, and in varying degrees still exists. Yet Nottinghamshire's long history of human activity offers ecological situations where it has so overlaid or channelled underlying natural forces, that some new classifications may be worth exploring. Wouldn't most natural historians and conservationists agree that human disturbance and chemical pollution are probably the two most important influences on modern habitats? It is precisely the reduced impact that human disturbance and chemical pollution have had on these private estate lands, by comparison with any other extensive tracts in this county, that give the Dukeries a wildlife importance.

The Dukeries proper (so-called because at one time during the 18th century five Dukes had properties there, and generally assumed to include the estates of Welbeck, Thoresby, Clumber, Rufford and Worksop Manor) covers an area to the north and east of Mansfield. Considered as a habitat rather than as an historical feature, the term is used as shorthand for areas of land inside the whole county (though particularly in Old Sherwood) which have been protected and created inside private estates and parklands — even though Clumber (National Trust), Rufford (County Council), Wollaton and Newstead Abbey (Nottingham City Council) have come into the public domain since the War. In fact if we consider the history of Sherwood as a protected area, the extension of this protection into modern times is entirely due to the great private owners, because the Crown disposed of its rights (and therefore Forest Law) between 1793 and 1818. Even long before this date it is clear that unspoiled, unfarmed Sherwood Forest was a prime area for the country seats of the great families of the realm, and great parks had been created. The following description by a Duchess of Newcastle shortly after the Civil Wars of the 17th century provides some interesting details of the wildlife that prospered as a result:

'Of eight parks which my lord had before the wars, there was but one left which was not destroyed, viz., Welbeck Park. The rest of the parks were totally destroyed, both wood, pales, and deer; amongst which was also Clipston Park, of seven miles compass, wherein my lord had taken much delight formerly, it being rich of wood, and containing the greatest and tallest timber of all

45

the woods he had; ... It was watered by a pleasant river that runs through it, full of fish and otters; was well stocked with deer, full of hares, and had great store of partridges, poots, pheasants, etc., besides all sorts of water fowl; so that the park afforded all manner of sports, for hunting, hawking, coursing, fishing etc., for which my lord esteemed it very much: . . . However, he patiently bore what could not be helped, and gave present orders for the cutting down of some wood that was still left him in a place near adjoining to repair it and gat from several friends deer to stock it.'

'Poot', incidentally, is not a mis-spelling of 'coot', but an old term for black grouse, birds which were still present in Nottinghamshire during the 19th century (as they were as late as the 1950s on Cannock Chase, and up to the present decade in Derbyshire), an interesting observation. The clear implication that they were common enough to shoot gives an idea of the birchy wildness of the area. It is impossible to consider the Dukeries without considering field sports. Whether or not we like it these areas have been maintained as sanctuaries partly, if not largely, so that wildlife and game could be preserved, enjoyed, and in some instances hunted or shot. Their guardian during years of increasing human pressure on the countryside has been the often hated gamekeeper. He may well have had a major hand in reducing the predatory bird population in Britain — for example, the buzzard is said to have recolonised most counties during the last War, when keepering was low. Mammal predators appear to have been more resilient: despite their control, some would say persecution, for at least a century on shooting grounds, overall populations of stoats, weasels and foxes have barely suffered, though in the past badgers may have done so in Nottinghamshire. The strange prejudices supposedly held by gamekeepers appear well illustrated by the only record in Britain of an Egyptian nightjar, shot in Thieves Wood, then part of the Portland estate, on 23 June 1883 ... by a gamekeeper. The event was recorded (and indeed commemorated with an inscription stone, since broken) by the eminent local natural historian, Joseph Whitaker. It is worth noting that the gamekeeper took the bird to Whitaker, and that most of the eminent natural historians of the day saw it as part of their own craft to shoot and obtain rare bird specimens. So this little Nottinghamshire record may project the gamekeeper as an interested observer of nature as well as a killer of species he (and his employer) view as needful of control. Today's gamekeeper (nearly an endangered species himself) is often tolerant of all but the most persistent, individual birds of prey. Nottinghamshire has a high kestrel, sparrowhawk and tawny owl population. Other species sometimes seen – such as buzzard, honey buzzard, goshawk, hobby, merlin, osprey, hen harrier and short-eared owl, are probably only visitors or occasional breeders. There are token breeding populations of little owl, barn owl and long-eared owl.

Of those species which have survived through human protection the foremost are deer. Present deer populations in Nottinghamshire are almost entirely due to such protection on private sporting estates; they are still mostly found in close association with them. The main species of deer at Sherwood have always been red and fallow. Roe deer were never popular on Royal Forests, presumably because they distracted the dogs during a hunt. They are not recorded at Sherwood beyond the 13th century. Their present recolonisation of the county, which has been taking place since around 1980 from the north, bridges a gap of 700 years. It is attributable, not only to legal protection since the Deer Act of 1963, but also to the increase in young tree plantations, which afford them the sort of close habitat they favour. In 1987 there are probably less than 40 of this species in Nottinghamshire but, because they produce two young a year and are family-based (unlike red and fallow which can only survive in a largish herd-area), they are capable of explosive expansion into uncolonised habitat. Nottinghamshire is not ready-made for roe, however, and it is likely that the main areas to be colonised will be woodland in Sherwood and the Dukeries, and also the more fertile farmland to the east of the county, with its hedges and copses. Wherever they come, this small and pretty deer (grey in winter, foxy-red in summer, and appearing tail-less above a white or buff 'tail-patch' on the backside) will be a delightful addition.

46

It was around the native herds of red deer (or High Deer as they were frequently called by the medievals) and the extensive lands of Royal Demesne (such as those pertaining to the manor of Mansfield) that the original system of court-supporting Royal Forests was conceived by William the Conqueror. The Anglo-Saxon Chronicle of 1087 suggests that 'He loved the High Deer as if he were their father', and it is easy to understand a deep love for these stately animals, which can weigh up to 227 kilos (500 lbs), but drift like shadows. The herds were probably already greatly reduced by the 16th century, when the first censuses were taken, but these still suggest 2/5000 red deer, plus well over 1,000 fallow!

The pretty roe deer is beginning to recolonise Nottinghamshire. (WE)

Here then was the raw material of deer stocks on which the large private estates worked, although there may well have been further introductions after the Civil War. The crucial period when the Dukery estates secured the survival of Sherwood's deer begins in the 18th century. Then the wealth to be made from improved agricultural techniques made deer no longer acceptable as wild animals, ranging the country and free to plunder crops. A 1708 petition to Parliament sets the tone, in which the Gentlemen of the North of the County of Nottinghamshire complain about 'the grievous almost intolerable burden we labour under by reason of the numerous increase of the red deer' to numbers approaching 1,000. Moreover, they alleged that the Forest Keepers 'threaten them if they so much as do set a little dog at the deer though in the corn'. Clearly this was a serious version of the perennial complaint of farmers against wildlife, and economic forces were such that something had to give. The solution that gradually emerged during the 18th century was the total imparkment of the deer on the great estates of the Dukeries. The costs for this were not entirely borne by the great landowners in all cases; the Duke of Newcastle-under-Lyme managed to persuade Queen Anne to defray much of his expense in building Clumber Park. However, when we speak of parks, the deer must have run semi-wild there. Thoresby Park, running to at least 690 hectares (1,700 acres) would have been typical.

47

Though many other animal groups have suffered in the 20th century it has been an important and rather successful age for the deer populations of Britain. Two things happened simultaneously in Nottinghamshire and elsewhere — the big estates have declined, and the deer parks in particular were broken down and never replaced in the World Wars; on the other hand huge areas have been re-afforested, by the Forestry Commission and others. Result: wild deer.

The fallow and red deer that spent the 19th and early 20th centuries on the great parks escaped in sufficient numbers to form breeding nuclei in the wild, and the territorial roe deer has spread through the country from Scotland in the north and a few small herds in the south. Fortunately this opportunity to have wild deer again has been seized, by protective legislation and modern deer-management. In particular, the high-powered rifle acts as a selective control of deer on farmland and other areas where too great a concentration would be unacceptable and has allowed wild deer and economic farming to live together for the first time. It is also better than the 'little dog' of the 18th century, because it is much more likely to succeed in conserving wild deer, which the little dog failed to do. Culling must be seen as a conservation measure, as history demonstrates, and to deplore it sentimentally is a luxury that conservationists cannot afford, if they wish to preserve deer stocks.

Nottinghamshire's deer are by no means numerous compared with other counties. Red deer are unlikely to exceed dozens in the whole county, so that when people see a deer it will invariably be the middle-sized fallow. Yet it is gratifying that such historically (and genetically) important strains as the red deer of Sherwood and the pure white fallow of Welbeck have been preserved and can still be glimpsed in their traditional habitats of oak and fern. Indeed, to come across a white fallow in the woods at dusk is to be transported back to the Age of Legend. Equally interesting for the naturalist is to discover one of the boggy areas in which the red deer wallow, and have probably wallowed for hundreds of years; or to see a small group of the pretty new-comer, roe deer, hesitate on the edge of a young plantation. Where deer can be seen in Nottinghamshire they are invariably popular with local people, well-managed and unharrassed, a fact which is reflected in their unusually good body weights and condition. This seems only right and proper for the deer of Sherwood, which have survived the twists and turns of human usage in the county, and which feature in both the badge of the Nottinghamshire Trust for Nature Conservation and the heraldic emblem of the county itself. It is to be hoped that deer will not be neglected in future land-development.

The importance of what remains of the landed estates is still as great as ever to deer. During the last ten years a particular study of fallow deer, based on those at Sherwood, has been undertaken. The central purpose has been to understand the biology and behaviour of fallow as a means to conserving them, and undoubtedly the main conclusion on behaviour is that fallow (and probably other deer species) can adapt their natural behaviour to modern countryside conditions provided they have one thing: somewhere secluded and undisturbed within the main range of the herd, where the does feel they have the security to give birth to their fawns. It is undoubtedly for this reason that, of the three fallow deer herds and one red deer herd living wild in the county, all but one are associated with keepered private estates, and the other is on a huge block of forestry land which is also wardened. In this age of countryside access and continuing decline of the old landed estates are we going to be sufficiently provident and self-restrained to provide areas of *seclusion* as well as habitat for wildlife? If we do, we will have acknowledged the Dukeries as a habitat.

Apart from deer, and the ancient oaks themselves what else has survived on the Dukeries? The Marquis of Manvers, exhibiting a then slightly eccentric view which we may see as an early form of conservationism, decided to leave the oaks standing when Crown protection had been removed. The Duchess of Newcastle described 'all sorts of water fowl'. The lakes at Thoresby, Welbeck and Clumber are the most important sanctuaries for both breeding and winter duck populations for many miles around, with teal, pochard, gadwall, shoveler, goosander and the recently naturalised

LEFT: The nuthatch enjoys the productive habitat of Dukeries parkland (DS) RIGHT: . . . as does the common long-eared bat. (DW) BELOW: The Trent at Attenborough, with a colourful show of purple loosestrife. (M&DG)

PLATE III

ABOVE: A grey heron was adopted as the symbol of the Nottinghamshire Wildlife Appeal. (DS) LEFT: Cinnabar moths frequent the side of the Trent. Here, their caterpillars feed on ragwort. (M&DG) CENTRE: The gatekeeper is a regular towpath companion for Trentside walkers. (M&DG) BELOW: The grass snake can still be found around canals and other streams. (DW)

PLATE IV

ruddy duck amongst others. (More problematical is the almost indisputably over-large Canada goose population which has built up in thousands on and near these lakes.) Although the actual dates of construction of the lakes is uncertain, they certainly pre-date the Repton era of landscaping, and as a consequence hold some interesting marshland and lakeside flora as well. Thoresby lake is particularly important in this respect. Many species of rush and reeds, such as sweet flag, Norfolk reed, reed-mace, reed canary-grass and some fine strands of sedge, including greater tussock sedge, and other plants of importance such as gypsywort and skullcap, are present, as well as significant populations of reed warblers and other water-edge birds, including water rails in the winter months.

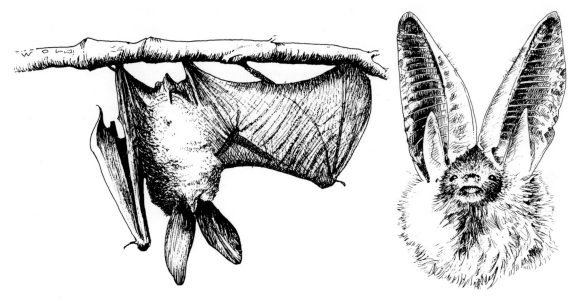

The common long-eared bat is just one of the bat species that enjoy conditions in the Dukeries. (WE)

Old parkland, like the lakes, deserves closer consideration as an important habitat. The old trees, both ancient oaks and parkland ornamentals (lime, yew, sycamore, Scots pine, Wellingtonia, sweet chestnut, cedar and beech are all represented with fine specimens) are the main, possibly only, stronghold for three bird species in the county: nuthatch, treecreeper and lesser spotted woodpecker. Parkland appears to show at least one example of an ecological 'special relationship' with the deer, in the presence at Thoresby Park of the flower houndstongue, whose bur seed is presumably transported on the fur of the deer, while the plant with its dark red flower is apparently poisonous, and never eaten. Today the old open trees are usually combined on these estates with conifer plantations, and this combination produces a place for hawfinch as well as crossbill, spotted flycatcher, redpoll, green woodpecker and woodcock. Visitors to the Dukeries are usually struck by the exceptionally high jay populations, and if Nottinghamshire were seeking a bird emblem, this would be a good candidate.

One other animal group which deserves special consideration in relation to both habitats of the Dukeries is bats. If Nottinghamshire has an interesting bat population then it is undoubtedly here. Bat numbers in Britain have crashed to 2% of the levels of 50 years ago, and the single most important factor in this crash is the reduction and pollution of insect populations by chemical insecticide on farmland and elsewhere, given the fine metabolic energy equation that bats depend on in their breeding cycle. In 1986 a conference on bat studies was held at Nottingham, and one paper from Scotland demonstrated the close association between good bat populations and the sporting and fishing estates which have been left unfarmed and unsprayed. The same is patently true in Nottinghamshire, where genuinely large populations of bats may be seen in the evenings over the Dukeries lakes. It is not difficult to understand why. The lakes and the surrounding parklands in particular have never been subjected to the chemical pollution which is the norm throughout the rest of the county and country. As luck would have it, these parklands and the surrounding woods also offer precisely the sort of ancient tree (not to mention ice-houses and the like) which several species of bat favour or even require for roosting, and which are completely lacking in modern forestry plantations, however extensive. As yet it is not at all certain how many bat species are present, as in Nottinghamshire as elsewhere this group has been poorly recorded, though large noctule populations are known to be present, as well as Daubenton's whiskered, long-eared and the ubiquitous pipistrelle.

It is a most exciting thing to find a noisy group of several dozen noctules emerging from what appears to be merely a twist rather than a crack in the bough of an ancient oak of Sherwood. And it is worth considering that, where bats have prospered, so very likely have species with similar requirements, such as moths and smaller (less conspicuous) insects, even if these are not fully recorded as yet. These are important factors in considering the management of these areas in future, and the real reason why there was such opposition recently to the idea of 'tidying up' Rufford Park by felling the old lime tree avenue. These areas have been handed to us as wildlife reserves of importance, because of their ancient, unpolluted, and in places protected habitat; this must not be thrown away, as many of the old estates move towards increasing use as public recreation spots. Certainly the National Trust at Clumber have recognised this responsibility by adopting a sensible 'zoning' policy to protect the most important wildlife areas from vehicles and other unacceptable over-pressure.

A visit to the Dukeries leaves an impression of old oak and birch alongside fine ornamental parkland trees, bracken, heather, acid grassland, conifer plantation and lakes. Deer, bat, nightjar, jay and great crested grebe are amongst the more distinctive species with a liking for this combination, a view shared by at least one well-known conservationist, Phil Drabble, who writes in *The New Shell Guide to England*: 'But the charm and individuality of Nottingham are in Sherwood Forest and the Dukeries'.

The green woodpecker, or yaffle, benefits from the Dukeries' parkland.
(KM)

ABOVE: Canada geese and other wildfowl on the ice at Rufford Park. (M&DG) BELOW: A handsome drake teal, smallest of the surface-feeding ducks. (M&DG)

51

ABOVE: Pochards in the swim. (M&DG) LEFT: Sweet flag grows around the Dukeries' lakes. (RHH) RIGHT: A tree creeper carefully searches for food.(JW)

LEFT: A close encounter with a noctule bat. (DW) RIGHT: Jays are noisy and colourful birds, commonly found in the Dukeries. (DS) BELOW: A woodcock demonstrates its amazing camouflage. (JF)

The population of Canada geese in Nottinghamshire has been very carefully
monitored, involving well organised annual round-ups. (NTNC)

Trent and Tributaries

(KM)

The Vale of Trent is an important feature of the topography of Nottinghamshire, due both to the river itself and also to the wide, flat valley edged in the main by small, yet often steeply inclined hills, which are sometimes pleasingly wooded. The present river goes back to the close of the Ice Age and the wide meanders and great width of the valley, often 3.2km or two miles, were formed by a more powerful, greater flow during some tremendous period of thawing.

Where the Trent enters the county at Attenborough, the level is 27 metres (90 feet) above sea level and the gradient falls gradually to 4.2 metres (14 feet) at West Stockwith at Nottinghamshire's northern boundary. This is a fall of 23.2 metres (76 feet) in 80.5km (50 miles), excluding the meanders of the river, which would add approximately another 32.2km (20 miles).

The Trent is tidal as far as the Cromwell weir, this stretch suffering at times both from flooding caused by excessive rainwater and from high tidal flow. There was a time when the Trent broke its banks four times a year on average, a natural occurrence which ensured that the farming close to the river was of stock on prime water meadows. Since the Second World War, modifications involving floodbanks, the isolation of the Colwick Loop and the building of the sluices there, plus the deepening of many minor streams have increased the speed of drainage. The Trent still floods at times of melting snow or during periods of exceptionally heavy rain, when it is contained by a system of washlands, ensuring that little harm ensues.The total catchment area of the river is over 10,360 sq km (4,000 sq miles) of which Nottinghamshire forms about one third. Part of the western boundary is marked by the River Erewash flowing south, bringing industrial pollution, and by the River Soar, a cleaner stream which drains much of the Charnwood Forest. Another main drainage system is the River Idle, with well known feeders, the Maun, Meden, Poulter and Ryton, which reaches the Trent at West Stockwith. Apart from the River Devon, fed by streams draining the south-eastern area of the county and joining the Trent at Newark, there are innumerable streams which flow directly into the Trent, such as the Dover Beck and the Greet. Some of these streams have created steep-sided ravines in the marl, clothed with bushes and trees, which provide cover and natural conditions for wildlife, more or less excluded from the surrounding farmland. These ravines are known as dumbles in Nottinghamshire, and in them can be found ferns enjoying the shady conditions, and various wild flowers, especially woodland species such as the bluebell, primrose, yellow archangel, greater stitchwort and wood garlic. Among the hawthorns, elders and other low trees, guelder rose can be found. This mixed linear woodland, with the stream providing essential water, is a quiet retreat for many species of birds throughout the year including hawks, woodcock, woodpeckers, doves, tits, warblers and finches.

A river, from a wildlife point of view, is only as good as the quality of water flowing into it and, in this respect, the Nottinghamshire Trent has never been as polluted as, say, the lower Thames. This was mainly due to the plentiful supply of clean water from Derbyshire brought by the Rivers Dove and Derwent. Praise should also go to the Nottingham City authorities who developed an efficient sewage system, beginning in the 1880s. The worst pollution came from the River Tame , along which the horrors of the industrial West Midlands were fed largely unchecked into the Trent system for decade after decade. It is only in recent years that a really serious attempt has been made to improve this abysmal 'hiccough', still continuing from excesses of the 19th century .

Watercourse	Location of Reach	1952/57 Quality	1984/85 Quality
River Trent	Attenborough to West Stockwith	B	2
River Erewash	Notts. border to R. Trent	D	3
Fairham Brook	Widmerpool to R. Trent	B then C	2
River Leen	Source to confluence with the Day Brook	B	1B
	Day Brook to R. Trent	C	2
Dover Beck	Confluence with Oxton Dumble to R. Trent	B	1B
River Greet	Source to R. Trent	A	1B
The Beck	Kneesall to R. Trent	A	1B
River Devon	Below source to R. Trent	B	1B
River Smite	Below source to R. Devon	B	1B
River Maun	Source to inlet, King's Mill Res.	C	1B
	King's Mill Res.	C	3
	King's Mill Res. to Mansfield	B	2
	Mansfield to Clipstone	B	3
	Clipstone to nr. West Drayton	B	2
River Idle	Nr. West Drayton to above Misterton	C	2
	Misterton to R. Trent	B	1B
Rainworth Water	Rainworth to Bilsthorpe	E	3
	Bilsthorpe to Gallow Hole Dyke	E	3
	Gallow Hole Dyke to R. Maun	E	2
River Meden	Below source to confluence with Skegby Brook	B	1B
	Skegby Brook to below Pleasley Hill	B	3
	Below Pleasley Hill to above Thoresby Lake	B	2
	Thoresby Lake to confluence with R. Maun	B	1B
River Poulter	Scarcliffe to R. Idle	A then B	1B
River Ryton	Source to Worksop	B	1B
	Worksop to above Ranby	B	2
	Above Ranby to R. Idle	B	1B

Key:

Grade   *1952-1957*

A.   Pure enough for trout and grayling and for caddis and mayflies.

B.   Clean enough for chub, dace and roach also water shrimps.

C.   Suitable for roach and gudgeon and for loglice and leeches.

D.   Strongly polluted. No fish, but bloodworms.

E.   Barren. Heavily polluted. Some fungus and tubifex worms in places.

Class   *1984-1985*

1A.   High quality water, high amenity value, game or high class fisheries.

1B.   Water of less high quality than 1A, but usable for substantially the same purposes.

2.   Drinkable after advanced treatment, moderate amenity value, reasonably good coarse fisheries.

3.   Water pollution to an extent that fish are absent or only sporadically present.

4.   Water grossly polluted and likely to cause nuisance.

The table shows the quality of local waterways as categorised by the water authority; the letter shows the grading for 1952—1957, while the number is the class of cleanliness updated to 1984—1985. For example, the River Ryton is shown as B for 1952—1957 and 1/2 for 1984—1985, which is some improvement.

From this table the following can be gleaned: improved — Rivers Leen, Devon, Smite, Poulter, Dover Beck; some improvement/mainly improved — Fairham Brook, Rainworth Water, River Ryton; no change overall — Rivers Trent, Erewash; slight deterioration, especially at head waters — River Greet, The Beck and probably other streams from the Mercia Mudstone to the Trent. These are standards at 1984—1985 and the objectives of the Severn Trent Water Authority are to improve them still further. Since 1975, especially below Nottingham, there has been a lusher aquatic plant life, which acts as a source of food for water creatures and, in turn, a support for the varied fish of the river. Anglers come great distances for club and national contests, often numbering hundreds on big match days. The fish of the River Trent and its tributaries represent a rich but often overlooked element of the nature of Nottinghamshire. Indeed, despite the history of pollution in many local waters, there is now throughout the county a greater diversity of species and, quite simply, many more fish alive than was the case fifty years ago. (This is particularly so because of the extraction of sand and gravel from the flood plain of the Trent. The resulting pits have made an ideal habitat for most species of fish.) Within the Trent and its tributaries can be found varied and fascinating populations of fish. At the smallest end of the spectrum is the three spined stickleback, which is to be observed so often in the jamjars of our youngest fishermen. It is an important little fish, because it forms the prey for many others, as well as for kingfishers. Another small fish, the minnow, is also a food species for larger fish such as chub, perch, pike and trout. It is at home in well oxygenated, running water and typical minnow habitats are afforded by the rivers Smite and Devon, which eventually flow into the Trent at Newark. Other common small fish include the gudgeon, with its single barbel on each side of its mouth, and the bleak, a slender fish which feeds at the surface of the water upon the larvae of insects such as midges.

The rudd, said by many to be the most attractive in the list of native fish species, does well along the fringes of naturalised gravel pits, but also shows up in the Trent. There can be few waters in Nottinghamshire which do not have a population of roach, because they are at home in the tiniest of farm ponds and in the strong flow of the river. Its success may rest upon its wide diet, which includes the larvae of insects, vegetable matter, the fry of other fish and algae which it finds on submerged stones. Large shoals of bream can also be found, wandering always, some think, to a particular browsing and feeding pattern. They grow to weights of more than 5 kilos (11 lbs) in ideal circumstances, but an average at a local level would be 2 kilos (4.4 lbs) or more.

Most of the species described so far have been silver/gold in appearance, but the tench is entirely different. It is generally green, although sometimes bronze. It also has the distinctive feature of a pair of small red eyes. The story of the barbel is one of a successful comeback. It was once prolific in the Trent before pollution from the Industrial Revolution killed it off. As a species it requires clean, strong-flowing water to survive, and so its comeback should be regarded as a welcome sign of a healthier environment. A thoroughly successful fish is the chub, which seems to outnumber other species in the Trent. It feeds across a broader range of temperatures than many fish, and is a great favourite with anglers.

The carp is now common in the county in both still and running waters. There are three varieties: the common, which is a fully scaled fish, the mirror, which has rows of scales about the size of ten pence pieces along its sides, and the leather, which has no scales. They are all represented in the Trent. There was, at one time, only a number of localised populations at the outfalls of the power stations which line the river. However, following two hot summers, the temperature of the whole river was raised to such an extent that the spawning rate of the fish was very high. They are now thriving, and there are fish from one kilo (2.2 lbs) to 10 kilos (22 lbs) distributed throughout the length of the river.

For many people, the salmon is a fish of romance and adventure. Not even the salmon, however, could clear the barrier of polluted water that was sent down the Trent for far too many years. The picture may be changing and there is no doubt that salmon are now trying to find their way up the river. They certainly reach the sluices at Holme Pierrepont, but it remains to be seen if they will get any further. It is possible that the new canoe slalom course may provide an alternative route. In May 1986, the Severn-Trent Water Authority announced that it was considering introducing salmon into the river in the wake of declining pollution.

Lastly, and such a long way from the stickleback, comes the pike — the supreme predator. After its first year it lives upon other fish, ducklings, voles, frogs and even fully grown water fowl. A weight of 13 kilos (28.6 lbs) is quite possible as an upper limit for any of the larger waters in the area. Long, green, mean and dangerous looking, it makes a fitting species with which to conclude this look at some of the fish of the county.

The water plants and animal life of the Trent, besides feeding the fish, also prove an attraction for waterfowl, which can be seen even in mild weather, whereas only the moorhen was seen regularly in earlier decades when other water was free from ice. The great crested grebe has bred on the river, using overhanging and partly submerged willow branches to make a secure nest. The mute swan has been unfortunate: the river's plant food has been a great attraction but, in the heavily fished areas, anglers' discarded lead weights have caused many slow, miserable deaths. The swan does not pass the weights through its system and, once locked in its gizzard (an organ where food is ground up), the weights slowly dissolve, causing lead poisoning. The new legal prohibition of the import or sale of lead weights between 0.6 grammes and 56.7 grammes (2 oz) may begin to reduce this danger.

The decision to build a chain of power stations beside the Trent (for example at Willington, Ratcliffe on Soar, High Marnham and Cottam) produced an unexpected bonus from the extraction of river water for the giant cooling towers. When returned warm, it raised the temperature of the water, not always a good thing in a hot summer, but a boon during long, cold spells. In really severe weather, when ice covers most waters, the Trent becomes a life-saver for many species of birds. The sawbills, goosander, red-breasted merganser and the smaller, attractive smew move up and down the river seeking the quieter regions, or where the flow is less strong. From the inhospitable North Sea come the divers — red-throated, black-throated and great northern which, when a thaw arrives, will take to nearby waters. The little grebe and great crested grebe are joined by the less common trio of the black-necked, slavonian and red-necked grebes, which compete for fish and other morsels with the kingfisher and the paddling heron. Goldeneye increase and scaup appear, accompanying the regular diving ducks, pochard and tufted, which feed on aquatic plants or associated animal life. Winter fishing competitions must also suppply some maggots from the baited swims.

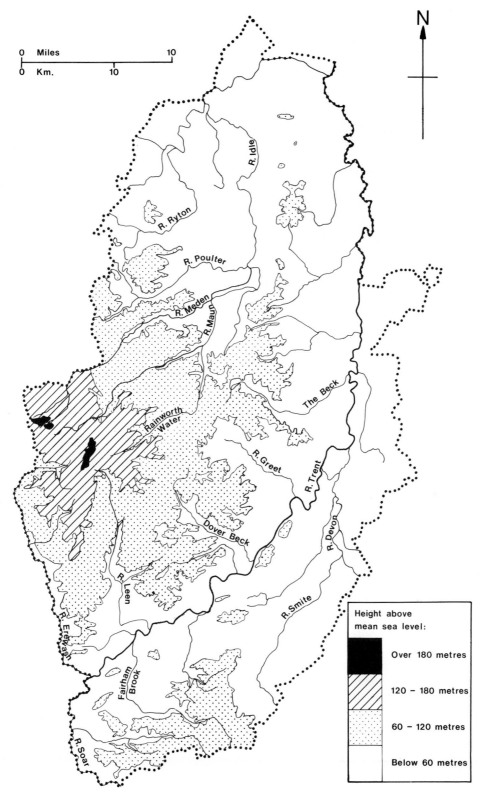

N

0   Miles   10
0   Km.   10

R. Idle

R. Ryton

R. Poulter

R. Meden

R. Maun

The Beck

Rainworth
Water

R. Greet

R. Trent

Dover Beck

R. Devon

R. Leen

R. Smite

R. Erewash

Fairham
Brook

R. Soar

Height above
mean sea level:

Over 180 metres

120 – 180 metres

60 – 120 metres

Below 60 metres

The main rivers and streams of Nottinghamshire.

Sadly, the otter is now only a visitor to the Trent (and to other Nottinghamshire waterways for that matter) and representation by the larger mammals rests with the common seal, which penetrates considerable distances upstream at times. A female had her pup well inland near Besthorpe in the 1970s and it was considered to have been successfully reared. The water vole is still present, especially on slow-flowing rivers. A careful approach to peep over a bridge parapet can sometimes catch one in the open, as it nibbles a succulent plant. Also present, but not often seen, is the water shrew.

The edges and tow paths of the Trent provide a linear habitat of unimproved grassland, where many flowers add grace and colour, growing almost undisturbed. In some places there is grazing by cattle and also some mowing in June, to accommodate the anglers, and this shorter grass assists the more prostrate flowers such as celandines and birdsfoot trefoil. Purple loosestrife, great willow herb, tansy and yellow toadflax have their show, and can be enjoyed on tow-path walks. Areas with pleasant surroundings, plus a good wildlife interest, include the north bank of the Trent from Beeston Weir and below Clifton Grove, and from Burton Joyce following the river round the great bend to Gunthorpe.

According to the seasons the wooded cliffs, which seem to hold the Trent on course, will vary from starkly black against snow, through the joyful greens of May and June and the heavier greens of full summer, to the hues of autumn. From April into summer there are the wild flowers to enjoy and, according to their times of flight, butterflies. The wall brown, meadow brown, skipper, gatekeeper, small tortoiseshell and peacock are regular tow-path companions on warm sunny days, while the painted lady and red admiral can be encountered. Most moths are nocturnal and in daylight hours are hidden away but, if gates and tree trunks are scrutinised, some can be found, such as the large, old lady moth which resembles a decaying leaf. The colourful six-spot burnet and the cinnabar moth, slow of flight and striking in colour, fly during the day, making for easy recognition. At times, in summer, they are joined by the unusual immigrant silvery, with its quivering wings.

If you are lucky during a walk, a kingfisher, concentrating on its fishing from an overhanging willow, can be surprised into flight, when its colour will out-shine those of the gaudiest butterfly. Black-headed gulls are regular Trent birds, either as commuters following the river or as hangers-on at fishing matches while, from May to September, the local common terns share the water, often performing a swift plunge for a small fish. Depending on the time of the year, the pied wagtail spends much time at the riverside and, at migration times, shares the little beaches with common sandpiper and meadow pipit.

A warning to anyone intending to walk a stretch of the river in late autumn and in winter: the open flatlands can be bleak, making it very much 'two sweater country'. Make sure to carry a warm drink or end the walk at one of the inns. Unfortunately, the miles of raised grassy flood banks which look like tiny examples of downland, do not contribute much to the natural life of the valley. Unlike downland they are not constructed with the chalk beloved of so many flowers, but rather, because of the work they must do, impervious clay. The grass is kept well mown to check the weeds and, apart from providing a home for the various soil fauna and a vantage point for the birdwatcher scanning the river, they are purely functional. The sowing of birdsfoot trefoil in this short grass would probably increase the population of the common blue butterfly. However, the washlands they contain are usually of pasture, providing feeding areas for the flocks of lapwing and often, their associates, the sad crying golden plover. Just as a flowing and then ebbing tide can inspire great activity among coastal birds, so does a Trent Valley flood among its local birds, especially after a severe freeze. Black-headed gulls quickly react and are joined by plovers, fieldfare, rooks and jackdaws, all seeking the worms and other grassland titbits. As if by telepathy, flocks of wigeon and teal congregate to exploit the shallow waters, and there are times when parties of both whooper and Bewick's swans join in. For wildlife, these washlands have increased

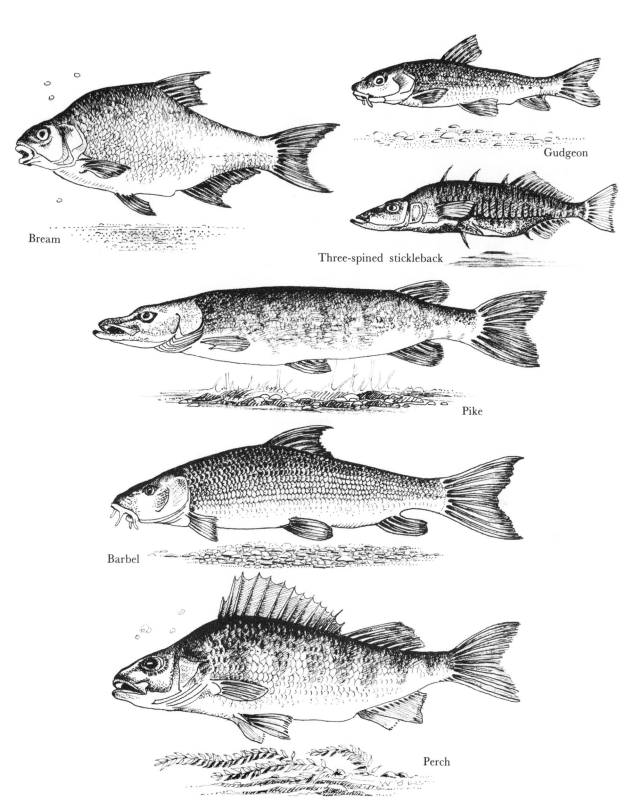

Bream

Gudgeon

Three-spined stickleback

Pike

Barbel

Perch

Some of the fish found in the Trent and its tributaries, (not drawn to scale).
(WE)

61

in value since the big change to intensive arable farming. For example, they remain a breeding area for the yellow wagtail and, in wetter patches, for snipe and redshank.

In earlier years, when drainage was limited, there were many patches of wetland fringed with reed, sweet grass and mace, and larger wet meadow areas called Ings. Mining subsidence at Dunkirk and Wilford added accidental marshes while the Nottingham Sewage Farm, stretching from the Netherfield railway sidings nearly to Gunthorpe, was a huge artificial marsh. One of the features of these wetlands, and especially the Nottingham Sewage Farm, was the opportunity to study waders. Twenty eight species were regular visitors and at least another eight were rare ones. The sight of a party of perhaps 22 greenshank coming into Burton Meadows, all calling loudly, enabled the watcher to feel the excitement of migration. Similarly, to witness the thrilling flight evolutions of a large flock of shore waders, comprising dunlin, little stint and curlew sandpiper, brought the North Sea coast to the Nottingham area.

On the Sewage Farm, a varied habitat of shallow lagoons, muddy patches, open water, moist grassland and, at Wilford and Dunkirk, the addition of wet meadows and flooded willow carr, provided suitable areas for all types of birds from grebe to wildfowl, from wader to marsh tern, and from owl to hirundine and bunting. Now, all this wetland is gone. (The demise of this old-fashioned method of sewage disposal took place from about 1960/61, with the last remnant at Bulcote.) One day conservationists will have to provide tired and hungry migrants with a new 'bed and breakfast' place. In the meantime, the development of the gravel industry and its gravel pits has temporarily saved the day.

Fortunately, many species still pass along the Trent Valley, especially during migration time or during hard-weather movements, giving local birdwatchers some exciting moments. As well as the gravel pits there are smaller waters along the valley, such as Wollaton Park Lake, Martin's Pond, Cromwell Fishing Pool and the Dunham, Coates, Cottam and Littleborough flood pools. All are 'windows on migration'. In their due season come the waders, the terns, scarcer gulls, seaduck and passerines, all attracted to fish, weed, insects or seed. Like Micawber, the birdwatcher hopes something unusual will turn up, and it often does.

To summarise, the Trent Valley, with its industrially created waters providing useful wetland; its country parks for water recreation giving aquatic habitats at least a limited chance to survive; its nature reserves and environmental patches such as Attenborough and Bleasby Pool providing a valuable sanctuary for many living things, and its grassy washlands usually free from the plough, add up to a natural asset of great significance. Through the valley flows the river, warm and genial, marking the migrant's highway on the north-east — south-west route to and from northern Europe.

Of the tributaries, the boundary rivers of the Soar and the Erewash have already been mentioned. In the south-east there is the Smite, the main tributary of the River Devon, which drains an area which has been described as an 'arable desert' due to intensively farmed fields and dredged-out streams, offering little in the way of variety or interest. There is the small, clean River Leen flowing down from the high ground above Newstead Abbey, and feeding the ponds and Abbey lakes on its way south through the Bestwood Country Park. Even though salt pollution from mine water has polluted the river on occasions, this is an attractive part of Nottinghamshire for the naturalist.

Further north, both the Maun and the Meden rise from the hills west of Mansfield which, together with the Poulter, provide watery habitats attracting considerable waterfowl to the Dukeries waters of Rufford, Thoresby, Welbeck Abbey, Carburton and Clumber Park. In recent years the osprey has made some long visits and also found the area congenial. The Ryton, rising to the west of Worksop, is another, similar river linking farmland, forest country and historical places (Osberton, Hodsock and Serlby). Flowing as they all do over the Sherwood Sandstone, these rivers carry insignificant amounts of water, considering the area they drain. They are all tributaries of the River Idle, which turns eastwards from Bawtry to join the Trent at West Stockwith. Sand and gravel extraction, such as at Lound, has enhanced and added variety to this area in the same way as it has to the Trent Valley. As with the Trent, all these rivers provide late-autumn into winter feeding areas for the graceful grey wagtail down from the hill streams, and for the attractive green sandpiper, a winter visitor from Scandinavia.

From Bawtry the River Idle drains the Carrlands, a name for the flat, low-lying area which represents the fenland or Holland of Nottinghamshire. As much of this land is less than three metres (10 feet) above sea level it has flooded many times in the past, creating a considerable layer of silt. Drainage was attempted by the Romans, and serious efforts were made in 1629, when Cornelius Vermuyden, a Dutch engineer, constructed the Morther (Mother) Drain. It was only partly successful, because it caused flooding elsewhere, and the Warping Drain north of the Idle eased matters only a little. A complicated system of drainage arose, ending in a network of channels and pumping stations which (to the delight of the birdwatchers of the era 1950—80) failed to check the flooding. In most years, after heavy rain or melting snow, the resulting huge area of water became a wildfowl refuge similar to the Ouse Washes. When not flooded, the pasture there provided good hunting for short and long eared owls, and for one or two hen harriers.

There was a considerable change from 1982, when a new drainage scheme came into operation, reducing dramatically the amount of water and the length of time that the land was flooded. Also, the efficient run-off caused land upstream as far as Scrooby and Mattersey to become drier. Needless to say, with the Common Agricultural Policy of the EEC operating, there followed an increase in arable farming and the usual decrease in the variety of wildlife. The high ground at Gringley village is a good vantage point to survey this low-lying land of hedgeless fields, dykes and dark alluvial soil. The Carrs still offer some wildfowl watching. Bewick's and whooper swans, for instance, seem to use the area as a staging post on their post winter migration. It is, however, unlikely that we shall see again the great gatherings of 1,700 pochards or the frequent flocks of 500/900 wigeon, as now it is very much a case of 'hurry there before the flood water quickly subsides'. Hen harriers and short eared owls still offer views of their differing hunting flights, and flocks of lapwing and golden plover find good feeding on the open land. Wheatears are regularly seen on the fallow or ploughed land at movement times and waders make brief halts. Dotterel have been seen and, in 1984, a lesser golden plover paid a visit, the first record of this species for Nottinghamshire.

Another watery habitat connected with streams and rivers is the canal. In Nottinghamshire this habitat is represented by the Chesterfield Canal, the Nottingham Canal, the Beeston Canal and the Grantham Canal. Tennyson spoke of 'haunts of Coot and Hern' in connection with his famous brook, but in places on these canals to the coot and heron can be added the little grebe, kingfisher, moorhen and the occasional mute swan. There are also peaceful stretches where, in summer, the humming of insects merges with the chatter of shy warblers — reed, sedge and whitethroat.

Coming into the county near Shirebrook, the Chesterfield Canal is a companion of the River Ryton, before leaving it north of Ranby to be near and just east of the Idle. Both canal and river swing east, almost meeting at West Stockwith. The Nottingham Canal, companion of the River Erewash, travels south and formerly passed through Wollaton to Nottingham, but it is now disused and ends near Wollaton. The short Beeston Canal is very much in use by small craft by-passing Beeston Weir. The Grantham Canal, once important for carrying coal and heavy goods to the villages of the Vale of Belvoir, offers some pleasing walks between the Trent and Grantham itself and, like the Trent, is a narrow, linear retreat for the various forms of life banished from arable fields by modern farming. Being of slow movement, the canals were and still are used for breeding by frog and toad, and their tadpoles may still be hunted by the grass snake, a great swimmer in the spring and summer, when it is easily seen. Other canal residents which enjoy these quiet back-waters are damselflies and dragonflies.

Except for the streams and rivers marred by pollution, water is a constant source of incidents to please the ear or eye. The sight of a party of black-tailed godwits heading north west and lifting over the Idle at Misson provides a share in the thrill of spring migration, whereas the dance of a damselfly around aquatic plants near the Burton Meadows captures the lazy days of summer. Seeing a spoonbill flying downstream and settling briefly at the shallow Dunham Pool is to enjoy a rare occurrence, but it in no way over-shadows the commonplace pleasure of hearing the wistful piping of a bullfinch blending with the song of lively dumble stream. The plop of a big fish rising to take an insect rouses the fisherman, just as the glimpse of a hawfinch while walking the Meden Trail in autumn pleases the birdwatcher.

These are just a few scenes from the riverside nature of Nottinghamshire and now, as the concern for wholesome water becomes general, and not just the interest of the conservationist, the future of our watery places brightens. Cleaner streams, fringed by cover, promise even more delights to come.

A peaceful morning by the Trent at Gunthorpe. (KM)

LEFT: Yellow archangel can be found in some of the dumbles that run towards the Trent. (RHH) RIGHT: Guelder rose can also be found in the dumbles. (RHH) BELOW: Minnows are an important food species for larger fish. (DW)

ABOVE LEFT: This mute swan with its cygnets may benefit from tighter control over the use of lead fishing weights (M&DG) RIGHT: The little grebe or dabchick is a fairly common resident in the county. (JF) CENTRE LEFT: A displaying drake goldeneye. (M&DG) RIGHT: A moorhen enjoys some Trentside sunshine. (DSm) BELOW: A water vole swims along the margin of a stream. (DW)

ABOVE: Angling is enormously popular along the Trent. (The cow is just an interested observer.) (STWA/VH) LEFT: A black headed gull in winter plumage. (M&DG) RIGHT: Graceful common terns can often be seen plunging into the water after fish. (M&DG)

LEFT: Celandines can be found along the Trent tow paths. (RHH)
RIGHT: Redshank still breed in the remaining wetter areas of the Trentside washlands. (M&DG) BELOW: The Chesterfield Canal at Drakeholes. (MB)

LEFT: In the summer reed warblers chatter in the vegetation along our waterways. (JF) ABOVE: The green sandpiper is an attractive winter visitor from Scandinavia. (M&DG) CENTRE: There have been reports that a female common seal had a pup in the Nottinghamshire Trent in the 1970s. Could a pup like this one possibly be the county's most unlikely mammal? (AG) BELOW: A juvenile grass snake shows off in front of a snail. (DW)

ABOVE: Bullfinches raise their young in a Nottinghamshire dumble. (JW)
BELOW: Staff of the Severn Trent Water Authority assess the fish
population of a stream using electro-fishing. (STWA/VH)

An aerial view of Ratcliffe-on-Soar power station, just one of the chain of Trent Valley power stations. The river Soar snakes its way past the power station to meet the Trent at the top of the picture. (NCC)

ABOVE: The coot is a common and often overlooked bird of the Trent Valley. (DS) BELOW: A view of the Carrlands near Misson. (NTNC)

Farmland

(KM)

The little village of Flawborough stands on a ridge of higher land, guarding the valley of the winding River Smite. Standing amongst the mellowed farm buildings, you can see across this fertile farmland a view which is at once unique to the village and yet so typical of the greater proportion of this agricultural county. Amidst the busy scene at harvest time the villages of Thoroton, Hawksworth, Scarrington and Aslockton tremble in a shimmering heat haze. Fields of waving wheat stems contrast with the sharp texture of the low-cut barley stubble, and all around stand stacks of bales waiting to be carted. From here it seems that every inch of space is used for the production of cereals, root crops, rape and grass. However, if you descend from the Flawborough hill and walk across the valley of the Smite to the Carr Dyke, and on again to the Roman Fosse Way, you will discover that the nature of Nottinghamshire finds a niche here, as elsewhere, in the fields of our farmland. During July and August, as the cereal harvest is gathered, the landscape changes quickly in colour, texture, and character. From the optimistic greens of young crops in the spring and early summer, the scenes change rapidly, through yellow and gold to the brown of the freshly turned ploughland. The harvest scene is pervaded by a sense of fulfilment, another year completed. But the farmers have no time to contemplate their achievements, because the next few weeks of preparation are critical to the success of the next crop.

The rigorous annual cycle of agriculture controls the seasonal landscapes and determines the wildlife of the farmland. Such familiar examples as the rook, the poppy, the bank vole and meadow brown butterfly are species which have lifestyles capable of surviving the perpetual business of farming, and some even take advantage of the food produced. Every acre of modern farmland represents an investment of 2,000 years of knowledge, skill and innovation. The object is to produce the maximum yield of one particular plant species at a time, to the exclusion of all others. Nature's attempts to intervene in this unnatural process result in farmland being intensively managed, and a highly competitive environment for wildlife. Ever since the first settlers brought their strains of giant wheat from Europe, farmers have had to apply all their resources to meet society's demand for food. Farming now can be more productive than ever, but the natural world has never been defeated. The increasingly difficult conditions faced by the native plants and animals have drastically reduced the number of wild species which can be found. However, some of those that do survive have flourished to become known as 'pests'; like the wood pigeon their populations have grown because they have adjusted to the changes, and no longer suffer the competition of other species forced to abandon the fields. Farmers have tried to eliminate a relatively small number of plants and animals which are harmful to crops or stock. In

73

so doing they have unintentionally reduced or removed other, harmless, species from the fields. The story is a continuing one, but it would be wrong to assume that the wildlife of Nottinghamshire's fields is the culmination of a progressive decline. There have been peaks and troughs, and new species have appeared on the scene to replace some of those which lost the battle to survive. Farming habitats will always change.

As the pressure to increase yield begins to slow down, many farmers welcome the opportunity to provide space for wildlife. There will always be exceptions, but the general trend is towards conservation, often creative conservation. Landowners are not just protecting and managing the wildlife they have, but increasingly introducing woodlands, rough land and wetlands to provide new habitats on agricultural areas. The annual cycle of farmland can be traced through history and across the county in a fascinating story which, at least, ought to inspire us to look afresh at a world of wildlife full of interest and value. Agricultural land, particularly in Nottinghamshire, has been dismissed by naturalists as uninteresting and unrewarding for too long. It is, in fact, not only the major user of land in the county but also an essential part of the life cycle of innumerable plants and animals, many of which may not readily be associated with the open fields.

At harvest time it is evident that farmers are not the only collectors of grain. All across the stubble and along the routes to the silos, barns and corn driers the spilled grain attracts birds and mammals. Some are obvious, and the ubiquitous flocks of wood pigeons indicate the success that this species has enjoyed, by supplementing its natural diet from the woodlands. This native bird of the wildwood stuffs its crop with the seeds of an alien plant grown on thousands of acres which once were covered with the wood pigeon's natural habitat of broadleaved, deciduous forest. The present day balance of fields and woods is critical; this species now relies on them both. No matter how much of a nuisance this bird may be, you have to admire its resourcefulness. Whether frightened off the fields by the artificial gunfire of gas cylinders or chased off the vegetables by the gardener each morning, the flapping wing beats and monotonous call of the pigeon are familiar, if sometimes unwelcome, sounds to us all.

The harvest mouse too has had to change its way of life. This agile and endearing little animal is not a wildwood native. It came to our fields, like the house mouse and the house sparrow, with the earliest farmers, a creature of grasslands, which found an easier way of life in the cereal fields of the past. Its name reflects a long standing association with our crops. Anyone who can remember watching or steering a reaper will know why this attractive rodent was so familiar, as it escaped, almost too late, running from the shelter of the stalks to take refuge in the standing stooks nearby. For centuries the harvest mouse built its nest in the corn, rearing its young in good time to allow them to disperse by the end of August. The extensive use of quicker growing, shorter stemmed cereal varieties denies the harvest mouse enough time to complete its breeding cycle. Now they can nest successfully only in reed beds, rough ground and overgrown headlands, where they find security for those vital extra weeks. Such suitable habitats are not easily found so, despite the substantial acreage of land under cultivation, this charming acrobat is now an uncommon sight on arable land. Where it does still breed in Nottinghamshire it can be seen, after the harvest, timidly scurrying from the cover of the headland or hedge to collect the spilt grain, a very different farmland character to the brash and extrovert wood pigeon.

The advance of autumn in the agricultural calendar means that, even on the drier, sandy soils of West Nottinghamshire, ploughing, harrowing and drilling are often completed by the end of September. Hedge cutting and ditching are finished before the first successive nights of frost. After all this frenetic activity in the fields, a long period relatively free from disturbance begins, as the nights grow longer and the temperatures drop. Peace and solitude reign over the miles of gently undulating arable land from north of Nottingham to Worksop. The fields are typical of later enclosures, with straight hedges around symmetrically regular field patterns. Most of the hedges are not of great age only being 150 years old. The number of woody species comprising the hedge structure is also restricted by the acidic, dry, light soils. Hawthorn dominates, often exclusively, holly and elder being the only other hedgerow shrubs found with any regularity. The few hedgerow trees tend to be oak and birch, and the headlands and road verges are a limited mixture of gorse, broom, bramble and coarse grasses.

If these sandland fields lack the rich variety of the claylands to the east and south, they do not disappoint a naturalist who knows where and how to find the plants and animals of this apparently meagre habitat. It would be surprising not to find a good population of skylarks, for these remarkable birds seem content to make their home almost anywhere. Their bubbling song encourages you to linger and listen for the calls of the specialist birds of the area. Whitethroat thrive in the shortcut hedges, especially where the bramble, gorse and elder thicken the tangle of low vegetation. Generally arriving in Nottinghamshire during the second and third weeks of April, four pairs of 'peggy' whitethroat will disperse over 40 hectares (100 acres) of the sandlands. Linnets also prefer these small, low hedges, and occupy the sandland arable hedgerows at up to twice the density of breeding whitethroat pairs. Linnets seem to favour gorse and birch cover, and feed in loose flocks, often with other finches, in autumn and spring.

Blackbird, dunnock, chaffinch, goldfinch and wren also occupy the more respectable hedgerows, but one of the most exciting finds for the bird watcher in this arable country is the corn bunting. Whilst it was a bird well known by 19th century bird watchers, this bulky, long-tailed bunting is seriously overlooked today. It tends to specialise in open arable land. Extensive wheat and barley fields suit it well, but do not attract the ornithologists. The true status of this species is yet to be established. Whilst it happily occupies the open country and must have increased its numbers with the increasing acreage of cereals, the corn bunting also needs a prominent song post. Telegraph wires and electricity lines have to substitute for trees. The art of corn bunting spotting is to sweep the binoculars along the lines of wires. Its song is not particularly melodious, but it is distinctive. So too is the flight silhouette, as the bird bounces across the top of the barley, often dangling both legs beneath its body.

Despite the sustained demand for barley from the breweries of Mansfield, Worksop and Nottingham, agriculture has had mixed fortunes on this light, dry land. Always the first area to be abandoned in the agricultural depressions of the 19th and 20th centuries, the thin top soil is particularly prone to blowing in spring. The roots of hedges stabilize the land and bind it with roots of the grasses which form an important part of each headland and verge. The grass tends to be tussocky, as on the associated heaths, and consequently shrews, voles and mice all find good cover in the hedges. Bank voles tend to feed in or close to the hedge, unlike the wood mouse, which will readily venture out into the field. Such sorties render these bright-eyed, long-tailed mice susceptible to aerial attack by kestrels, which are regularly seen hovering over arable land. If small mammals are not about, linnets and other finches are likely to add variety to the kestrel menu. Barn owls are still resident at some of the sandland farms too. They are encouraged to stay by farmers who recognise the privilege of protecting what is sadly now one of Nottinghamshire's rarest breeding predators. The remains of meals found around the barn owl residences indicate that they rely almost exclusively on the voles, mice and rats of the arable fields and the farmyard.

Weasels can still be found along the sandland hedgerows and in the often wide verges of roads across West Nottinghamshire. Stoats are much less common perhaps because of the decline in rabbits. However, other familiar residents of the sandland farms include common and red legged partridge, stock dove, carrion crow, jackdaw, meadow pipit and pied wagtail. The lack of surface water, except in the valleys of the Poulter, Meden and Maun, is another factor restricting the distribution of many plants and animals in this part of the county's farmland though, surprisingly, toads are not uncommon. Common lizards may occasionally be found basking on warm sandy banks in the summer sunshine. The dryness of soils and the restricted list of plant species eliminate many butterfly species regularly found elsewhere in Nottinghamshire. Common blue, small heath and small copper grace the hedges and banks, and many of the moths of dry, grassy heaths will wander onto the arable land.

Over the last 30 years the development of intensive poultry units tended to concentrate in West Nottinghamshire on the sandstones. The landscape was peppered with their low profile buildings, feed hoppers, bungalows and stores. From outside, there was little sign of the concentrated life within these units, except for the supply of feed which was invariably scattered around. This source of nutritious food was found by wild animals. Rats and mice were abundant unless strictly controlled, flocks of house and tree sparrows, starlings and finches all came to the poultry huts in winter. The main species to take early advantage of this supply, however, proved to be the collared dove. After a few 'invasions' it arrived on the East coast in the 1950s. Its spread across Lincolnshire into Nottinghamshire was remarkably fast and, at first during the 1960s, was strongly associated with the spread of poultry units, where the new arrivals were frequently seen to congregate. Collared doves soon occupied other niches in suburbia and Nottinghamshire's

maturing coniferous plantations. By the time the poultry units started to be closed and abandoned this coloniser was well established. It no longer needed the grain feed of the poultry to promote its seemingly irresistible progress into the county's natural history.

In the dampness of autumnal mists the roving flocks of finches on the fields grow steadily in size, as the countryside slows down for the long winter ahead. Farmland residents including house sparrow, chaffinch, greenfinch, goldfinch and linnet are joined by redpoll and tree sparrow, as winter visitors from the woodlands, and by brambling and siskin from the colder north. Such flocks also include smaller numbers of yellowhammer, reed bunting and occasionally twite and snow bunting if the weather turns really cold. Counting a one thousand strong band of these seed-eating wanderers is a chilly job for the birdwatcher, but the reward is in the knowledge that so many of our most colourful British birds are thriving. The seeds of grasses, thistles, teasels and other arable weeds are an important part of their success.

Stoats can be found along the sandland hedgerows of West Nottinghamshire. (WE)

The dispersal of finch flocks to the roost is a sudden event each day. One minute there are hundreds of birds to see, the next, they have gone in chattering, wheeling flocks of confusion to the woods, copses and hedgerows. The rook's return to roost is a more dignified procedure. For two hours or more these resourceful and intelligent crows slowly flap their way back to the woodland roost. Although they have probably been feeding alone, several miles from their night quarters, they join together in loose flocks, increasingly filling the evening sky with their laconic 'caw' and ominously black silhouettes. From their vantage points over the fields they wisely observe the activities of the farmland below. As they settle in the trees, the sense that these adaptable birds are privately discussing what we do is inescapable. Perhaps we should take more heed of what the rook could tell us. It must always have been a common bird on our farmland, so the fluctuations

76

in the number of breeding pairs in the rookeries have not been particularly noticeable until quite recent times. A rook census was first carried out in Nottinghamshire as early as 1928, and again in 1932 and 1944. On the first two counts over 6,000 pairs were recorded, with the notable increase to over 10,000 in 1944, when more land had been turned to arable use. The increase continued, and the 1958 census by the Trent Valley Bird Watchers recorded an encouraging 17,000 pairs. Again, this was no doubt the result of increasing cereal acreage. Only four years later another census recorded a serious loss, down to 10,600 pairs. This count followed the years 1959 to 1961 when poisonous seed dressings of the chlorinated hydrocarbon group (aldrin, dieldrin etc) were used extensively on Nottinghamshire's arable land. Dead rooks were found lying about the fields and beneath rookeries, in numbers which exceeded expected deaths through old age and other natural causes. We responded to the warning provided by the rooks then, and banned the use of these dangerous chemicals. But a new survey of rookeries in 1975 showed a continuing (18%) decline in the 1962 figures, down to only 8,700 pairs, this time for different reasons. Many well-known rookeries had been lost to urban development since the 1960s, including some at Bawtry, Newark, Mansfield and around Greater Nottingham. Woodlands and other groups of trees in the fields which the rooks relied on had been felled in the 1970s, during the enlargement of arable units to provide for increased use and efficiency of machinery. The rook was still regarded by a few as an agricultural pest, because the 1975 census recorded the deliberate destruction of some entire rookeries, as opposed to the usual culling by the winter shoot. The balance of factors affecting the success of the rook is complex and other influences also play a part. The rook population is steadily falling back to the lowest levels ever recorded, despite the increase in arable land which ought to suit the bird. Another rookery census, and a careful examination of the story which this species is telling us this time, may be a vital indication of the value of our present-day farmland for wildlife.

Rookeries are not evenly distributed throughout the county. There are concentrations of colonies on the farmlands of the extreme south and south-east of Nottinghamshire. Indeed, in the 1975 survey, a single 10km square based around Cotgrave and Owthorpe held 10% of the total number of nests in the county, and the largest single rookery — the only one with over 200 pairs. In contrast to the bare late autumn and winter scenes of the sandlands, this area of the south wolds, the Vale of Belvoir, and especially that part of south-east Nottinghamshire which lies close to the boundary with Leicestershire, are relatively greener. They have many more hedges and hedgerow trees and fields of permanent grass. A drive from Nottingham to the county boundary on the Melton Mowbray road passes through Hickling, Upper Broughton and a distinctive, rolling countryside of mixed arable, grassland, woods, copses, spinneys, hedgerows and byways, which provide wildlife with a winter home of shelter and security. These fields lie on the glacial boulder clays and the lias clays, where agriculture has retained a significant proportion of permanent grassland. Enclosed during the 18th century from the massive, arable, open fields, this landscape has not generally lost the extensive cover of hedgerows and trees, because the requirements of modern cultivating machinery are irrelevant here. Many of these fields boast the distinctive ridge and furrow of medieval ploughland, which was still there when, 200 years ago, the land was converted from arable to pasture. The fertile, if heavy, soils support a wide range of hedgerow shrubs, including blackthorn, buckthorn, elm, field maple, goat willow, and some of the finest displays of climbing dog and field rose species to be found in the county.

This is a subtle landscape of intimate character and a timeless quality which is fully appreciated on cold, clear days. A low winter sun will light the hills and hollows, and a soft cover of snow emphasises the roll of the ridge and furrow like ripples washing down each hillside. The fields may be dormant but they are full of potential. Beneath the snow the miniature life of the soil continues, with tiny predators feeding on innumerable and even tinier species of invertebrates which spend the winter in the damp, dark world of the soil. Leatherjackets overwinter in the soil beneath grasslands by the millions. If they survive the winter these larvae will become another generation of crane flies, known to us all as 'daddy long legs'. The larger larvae and other insects may be dug from the soil by badgers and, when other food is hard to find, by foxes. The fox is an important member of farmland wildlife society. Whilst it may be a cunning and wily predator, its presence has indirectly helped many other species to survive. Fox hunting across the North Leicestershire and South Nottinghamshire countryside has been an important part of the life of almost every farm in the area. Encouraging the fox to earth in coverts and spinneys, and providing small but regular patches of rough ground for its benefit has also provided habitats for a host of animals and plants which could not otherwise have survived in agricultural areas. Tracks in the snow across the South Nottinghamshire fields reveal that the fox is still at home in the farmland. He is not the only hunter/scavenger with a truly omnivorous appetite, for this is also magpie country. This striking member of the crow family has that remarkable skill of changing its behaviour to suit the circumstances. In this respect both fox and magpie are classic examples of woodland wildlife tenaciously holding their ground on farmland. Like a giant shrike, the magpie

Foxes are some of the great opportunists of the countryside, and important members of the farmland community. (WE)

ruthlessly hunts for small birds and mammals in the winter hedgerows. If these are scarce it will feed on the fruit of the shrubs or it will rummage its way through the leaf litter beneath, to pick out centipedes, beetles, worms and other invertebrates, trying to conceal themselves in the debris of the hedge bottom. The adaptability of the magpie has also led to its successful occupation of urban areas, but out in the countryside every 40 hectare (100 acre) farm is likely to support one or two resident pairs.

Here and there in Nottinghamshire can be found a small proportion of the once extensive fields of permanent grass which were flooded each year by artificial drains, springs or by natural streams over-topping their banks. The depletion of these special habitats has been the result of agricultural 'improvement' of the meadows to increase the grass yield by drainage, or the application of fertilisers and selective herbicides at the expense of the herb species which naturally grew well in the meadows. Some of the meadows are now nature reserves, farmed by the Nottinghamshire Trust for Nature Conservation, to ensure that their special botanical and entomological interest is protected. By March the snipe have started 'drumming' their buzzing song flights over the watery meadows, and for the next four months or so the fields change through a splendid, colourful cycle, provided by the sequence of blooms in the meadowland flora.

Beside the Caunton Beck lie 9 hectares (22 acres) of fine, traditional hay and grazing meadows. Once regularly flooded by the Beck, the fields are watered now only by springs, but after heavy rain, ponds appear on the surface to create a lush growth of grasses, rushes and sedges. The flowering plants include primrose, false oxlip, cowslip, violets, lady's smock, ragged robin, marsh marigold and several buttercup species, indeed many of the once familiar flowers which people remember when they visit the Eakring and Maplebeck Meadows reserve. The colour in these fields and the number of trees and hedges around the reserve contrasts sharply with the rising land to the south, where a single field stretches as far as the eye can see, without a hedgerow or flower in sight.

The meadows, though, are a botanist's delight and have many other surprises in store. Snipe, lapwing, mallard, moorhen, reed bunting and the occasional sedge warbler are attracted to nest on the reserve. The lesser whitethroat and its common relative frequently sing from the dense cover of the hedges, and from willow and hawthorn copses on the opposite bank, which are now managed as an integral part of the meadows. From early spring the fields have brimstone, orange tip and vanessid butterflies flitting across the low turf and along the hedges and stream bank. The butterfly population reaches a peak at hay time when 15 species are regularly recorded on this site. Numerically the meadow brown is most abundant, with 500 individuals often seen in just one of the four fields, dancing their way across the drying hay after it has been mown. Skippers are also common. These darting insects rely on the grass throughout their life cycle. Large and small skipper species can both be found, but are much more difficult to study because of their perfectly timed flight from advancing naturalists. The wall brown, however, will bask obligingly on the warmth of a stone, bare earth or gate post, wherever it can absorb the heat of the sun. Peacock, small tortoiseshell and red admirals will emerge from the nettle beds to feed, as adults, on thistle flowers, often in the company of cardinal beetles, burnet moths and several species of bees.

There are other meadow nature reserves managed by the Nottinghamshire Trust and each has its own range of plant and animal species to be taken into consideration as the sites continue to be farmed. Traditional cycles of grazing and mowing for hay are diligently pursued by the Trust to maintain their botanical interest. Ashton's Meadow near Retford celebrates spring with the flowers of 100,000 cowslips. Chilwell Meadow, on the outskirts of Nottingham, is a splendid demonstration of how traditional habitats, with all their associated species, can survive, if protected and managed, even when surrounded by new development in an urban area. A diligent search in this reserve can reveal plants such as marsh horsetail and the delicate but elusive adder's tongue fern. Teversal Pastures, near Skegby, are at their colourful best in late June and July with an outstanding range of species, including hayrattle, sorrel, common spotted orchid, ox eye daisy, clover, vetches, speedwell and many more. These remaining meadows protect representatives of the splendid variety of plants and animals once commonly found, before so many old meadows were 'improved', ploughed or otherwise destroyed. Every remaining meadow, whether a nature reserve or not, is an increasingly important part of our countryside heritage. They are irreplaceable in character and history, aesthetically beautiful and precious reservoirs which hold the last examples of wildlife communities, loved by everyone who knew the countryside of thirty years ago.

By midsummer the haymeadows have been mown and cleared, and the main interest switches to the wildlife of the surrounding hedgerows. The value of hedges to wildlife depends, in much the same way as it does for woodlands and ancient meadows, on their historical continuity. Some are extremely old, dating back to Saxon times, when the surrounding land was first cleared by the new villagers. The lanes and boundaries were edged with banks and ditches and then planted with the native shrubs from the surrounding woodland. The long list of woody species found in the ancient roadside hedge along the front of the Eakring and Maplebeck Meadows reserve reflects both its age and the complexity of the interdependent plant and animal communities. The oak and field maple support incomprehensible numbers of invertebrates, from wasps to weevils and moths to millipedes, at every level from the soil to the tips of the oaks' 'lammas' growth of fresh green summer foliage. The alder, hazel and ash produce prolific seeds for the birds, whilst the elder, hawthorn, holly, buckthorn, bullace and guelder rose produce their seeds in berries, to attract winter thrushes, and small mammals like the wood mouse and bank vole. Dog rose and field rose, bryony, woody nightshade and ivy scramble over the hedge, entwining further woody species, including wild privet and pear, elm and crab apple.

These ancient hedges of the claylands of Central Nottinghamshire are some of the richest in the Midlands and, although less than one in ten of all hedges are of this age, complexity and quality, there is usually at least one example in every parish, probably on the boundary or along or leading to the edge of the ancient parish woodlands. It is an encouraging sight to see farmers and indeed, teams of volunteers, working in the Nottinghamshire countryside, practising the art and craft of laying these old hedges to the traditional Midland bullock style. It is on this work that the future wildlife value of our hedges depends. Nowadays new planting probably balances hedgerow loss and, whilst some changes will always be made, the small proportion that are ancient hedges must remain intact. Hedgerows were always planted for a purpose, and that reason may have disappeared long ago. For every mile of hedge that stabilises soil there is a mile which heavily shades out a crop. For every advantageous insect resident there is a potential pest. The arguments for and against hedgerow removal should now concede that most are not of overriding agricultural merit but are of historic, aesthetic and wildlife value and that these are sound enough reasons for retaining the general balance we have today, which lies somewhere between the excessive cover of the early 19th century and the great plains of arable land which spread over the landscape of medieval Nottinghamshire.

This county has a unique example of the open field system of farming. Established by the Saxons 1,000 years ago, the great arable fields, divided into strips, were finally enclosed in most other parishes by 1850. In Laxton, though, the fields and the agricultural system which administers them, remain suffiently intact for us to appreciate the landscapes and wildlife of most of lowland England. On the ridge of the great South Field you are surrounded by a huge expanse of arable land with no sign of cover or division, except for one small parcel near the main access from Moorgate Common. Here a quirk of Laxton's peculiar history resulted in just one enclosure. On Mill Field and West Field too, hundreds of hectares of crops stretch to the parish boundary, devoid of cover, and occupied only by the birds and mammals which enjoy the wide open spaces. Hare and partridge are two such residents, rooks, crows and lapwing will glean the stubble in autumn, with wood pigeons and stock doves. But they are visitors only. Like most other farmland species they need the cover of rough ground, woodland or hedgerows for roosting and nesting. In medieval times, of course, woodland habitat was more extensive than it is today. Every parish managed a part of the former wildwood to produce the timber needed in large quantities on the farms. Enfolding stock whilst grazing on the open commons or the stubble required hundreds of metres of sound hazel hurdling cut from the coppiced woods. The medieval landscape did contain some hedges and a proportion of them survive today. They lined the main lanes to prevent stock from wandering onto the open fields or smallholdings of land behind the farm steadings. The parish and other important boundaries were also marked permanently with hedged ditches and banks. The enterprising hedgehog would have been familiar to Saxon and medieval farmers, as it trotted along on its nocturnal wanderings, seeking anything from small mammals and frogs to insects, or the eggs of birds which had occupied these ancient routes and boundaries. The landscapes of the open fields occupied most of this county (except the great forest of Sherwood) for about 1,000 years. We cannot be sure of the wildlife populations of those times. Even though the open fields lacked adequate cover for the animals, the relative inefficiency of farming then must have resulted in the crops being well coloured with the flowers of arable weeds such as poppies, corn marigold and cornflower. Additionally, there were many more 'primary' woods close by, with all the native woodland species. Hedges, if fewer, were no doubt richer in plants and animals. All of the open fields had hay plots within their boundaries, in which grassland plants and animals could thrive, as they do today, in the sykes of Laxton.

Of all the habitats of the county, farmland has always been the subject of greatest change. By its very nature it varies from year to year, from decade to decade. There is no advantage in attempting comparisons. Instead, we should examine more closely the potential of what we have. Every hedgerow could one day be an ancient hedge, richer and more attractive than today. Every field produces more than just the crop, and feeds others than those who pay for the meal. If species have been lost from farmland habitats as the result of minor changes in the past, then equally small adjustments in the practice of managing the whole farm unit could enable them to return. All over the county there is increasing evidence that the inevitable process of change is swinging once more towards the conservation of those species which can, with a little help, find a home amidst the thousands of hectares of productive agricultural land in Nottinghamshire.

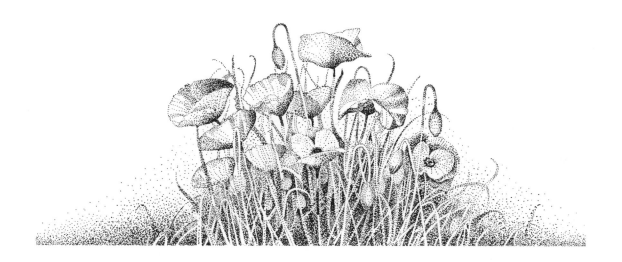

Poppies are some of the brightest of all our 'weeds'. (KM)

ABOVE: High technology harvesting. (M&DG) LEFT: The agile and endearing harvest mouse has found it difficult to adapt to modern farming methods. (DW) RIGHT: Barn owls are now one of Nottinghamshire's rarest breeding predators. (DS)

LEFT: The attractive goldfinch can be seen around farmland hedges. (DS)
RIGHT: Greenfinches are common farmland residents. (JF) BELOW: A
handsome cock pheasant is a striking inhabitant of farmland. (M&DG)

ABOVE LEFT: Blackthorn blossom and RIGHT: sloes, sought in the
autumn for making sloe gin. (M&DG) BELOW: Dog rose. (DSm)

LEFT: Field rose. (DSm) RIGHT: Wild roses. (MB) BELOW: A light
dusting of snow emphasises the roll of ridge and furrow. (M&DG)

ABOVE:A fox cub stares at an intruder.(DW) BELOW: A fox with its next meal. (DW)

ABOVE: Magpies fulfill their role as scavengers. (JF) LEFT: Ragged robin is just one of the once familiar flowers that can be enjoyed in the county's flower meadow nature reserves. (MB) CENTRE: Brimstone butterflies add beauty to the meadows from early spring. (DSm) RIGHT: An incredible 100,000 cowslips flourish at Ashton's Meadow nature reserve near Retford. (RHH) BELOW: Cadets of the Royal Air Force from Cranwell built a bridge for the Trust at Eakring Meadows nature reserve. (NTNC)

87

Urban Nottinghamshire is not a desert for wildlife but an ever-more appreciated network of productive habitats. (SM)

Urban Wildlife

(KM)

The urban and suburban habitats of roads, buildings, pathways, channelled waterways, playing fields, gardens, parks, cemeteries and derelict land, comprise some of the world's most artificial landscapes, brought about entirely for the convenience of the human inhabitants. Cities first appeared some 5,500 years ago, but they were small, and the majority of the population still lived and worked in the countryside. Today, towns and cities still occupy a relatively small area compared to the land mass as a whole, but they now contain high proportions of a region's total population. More than two-thirds of the population of Europe live in cities, and in Nottinghamshire more than a quarter of the county's residents live in the City of Nottingham alone.

Over the last two decades, interest in the natural history of the built environment has increased, and urban areas are no longer considered biological deserts. Indeed, with modern agriculture and forestry making rapid inroads into rural wildlife habitats, the value of urban open space as a refuge for nature has increased. Yet, despite the fact that most people associate our native plants and animals with the countryside, the fascination of observing wildlife on our own doorstep within the heart of the built environment is not diminished. It is as great a thrill to spot the blue flash of a kingfisher along a canal bank in the centre of Nottingham as it is to see one in more rural surroundings. Urban wild spaces are, however, not sacrosanct; few of those favoured by wildlife have any formal protection, and many are threatened by industrial and housing pressures. In the City of Nottingham, for example, several of the most valuable sites for wildlife are earmarked for future development.

Recognition of the wildlife value of open spaces in towns and cities has led to many exciting initiatives in urban conservation in Britain during the last 10 years and, in particular, the formation of urban wildlife groups. In 1984 a first step was taken by the City of Nottingham Group of the Nottinghamshire Trust for Nature Conservation, to increase its commitment to the protection and enhancement of Nottingham's urban wildlife: 1985 saw the start of a wildlife survey of the City and 1986 the inauguration of the Trust's Nottingham Urban Wildlife Scheme. Several sites are now being managed for their wildlife value, although conservation in the urban environment is not without its difficulties. This chapter concentrates largely on the survey of Nottingham's wildlife; similar animal and plant communities can be found in other towns in the county such as Mansfield, Newark and Retford.

The urban environment often supports a unique fauna and flora and cities, particularly older ones, usually contain a considerable variety of habitats, ranging from derelict land covered with tall weeds, to mature, well-established woodland. It is vacant 'wastelands'—the demolition sites,

89

rubbish dumps, industrial tips, gravel pits, railway tracks and embankments—which often provide the principal locations for wildlife. These disturbed sites vary in age, soil-type and size (from less than half a hectare—just over an acre—to more than 10 hectares or 25 acres), a variation which is reflected in the diverse wildlife which some of them support.

Other outstanding green areas in towns and cities are the open spaces occupied by natural, pre-urban vegetation or 'encapsulated countryside'. The distribution of these green areas reflects the pattern of urban development which has taken place. In Nottingham, the majority of rural habitats caught within the city are situated near to, or cross, the City boundary. This reflects the concentric pattern of urban growth, with expansion from the centre; as a consequence there are no large areas of encapsulated countryside near the City centre, the exception being Wollaton Park, which until 1925 was in private hands. Now over 220 hectares (550 acres) of the original parkland and woodland have been retained by Nottingham City Council, and the old Hall houses the Nottingham Natural History Museum. The future of this site as urban green space is ensured.

Green spaces are not the only urban wildlife areas for, within the built environment, artificially created habitats also occur in the form of walls, roofs and pavements, which reproduce a similar habitat to that of cliff and rock face. These man-made structures have allowed some species to increase their range of distribution in a dramatic fashion. For example, the small ivy-leaved toadflax can now be found climbing over shady walls and buildings well away from its native mountain habitats in the southern Alps and Balkan Peninsula. Likewise, feral domestic pigeons exploit office-block window sills for breeding sites, in the same way that rock doves, from which they are descended, favour the rock ledges of sea and mountain cliffs. Both pigeons and that other common urban resident, the starling, now fully exploit the urban environment, using city buildings and trees as roosting sites, and receiving much of their food from the human inhabitants. Roof-tops also provide a habitat for crustaceous lichens. Asbestos roofs are particularly favoured and may become covered in a mosaic of coloured patches. The most frequent species are *Xanthoria parietina*, which is bright orange when growing in full sunlight but yellow or green in the shade, and the mustard-yellow *Candelariella vitellina*. The abundance and distribution of lichens in urban areas can provide a living indicator of the cleanliness of the air.

In Nottingham, as in other large urban areas, conditions for wildlife are rather different from those pertaining in the surrounding countryside. For example, the temperature is higher, often by several degrees centigrade, and, although rainfall may also be higher, owing to increased cloud formation promoted by air pollution, humidity is generally lower. The warmer climate of cities results in fewer days of frost and snow and affects both animals and plants. Urban blackbirds may breed up to three weeks in advance of their rural counterparts, whilst the urban flora often contains species of a more southerly distribution. In the towns and cities of Nottinghamshire, several plants whose main distribution is in the drier and warmer areas of central and southern Europe can be found growing, such as annual wall rocket, fennel and lesser broomrape. Other species, which were originally planted into parks and gardens, have also successfully introduced themselves on waste ground. A widespread example is buddleia. Originally a native of China, buddleia, or 'butterfly bush' as it is also known, now grows successfully on urban wastelands, and attracts nectar-seeking butterflies, hoverflies and bumble-bees to its large bunches of purple flowers.

Intensive domestic and industrial activity has inevitably led to pollution of varying degrees: soils are compacted and may be contaminated with various waste products (for example, pulverised fuel ash near the old Wilford power station in Nottingham); noxious gases and dusts are expelled into the air, notably suphur dioxide from the combustion of fossil fuels, lead and carbon monoxide from traffic exhaust, plus dust from factories and incinerators; waterways are used as convenient waste disposal dumps—few urban ponds and rivers are without a rusty supermarket shopping trolley. Others contain less obvious but more insidious pollutants.

As a consequence of decades of air pollution, the abundance of simple plants (mosses, liverworts and lichens) has been dramatically reduced, and, although the air we breathe is now significantly cleaner than it was 20 or 30 years ago, cities do not usually support an abundant moss or lichen flora. The presence of lichens in cities provides a 'ready reckoner' of the levels of air pollution. Lichens which are, a close association of an alga and a fungus, are particularly susceptible to air pollution, so the more lichens the cleaner the air. Another factor limiting the distribution of these plants, and in particular the mosses and liverworts, is that they favour damp, humid habitats, which in dry, built-up areas are uncommon. Although a few places in Nottingham support communities of simple plants (the old gravestones in the shadier sections of the General Cemetery, for example) the species-diversity throughout the City is low.

Recent purification schemes by water authorities have led to the return of game fish to several of our major rivers, yet urban waterways are characterised by an impoverished aquatic wildlife. In Nottingham, sections of the River Leen have been culverted or canalised through concrete channels, inimical to wildlife. Along more natural sections, however, kingfishers dart, showing the tenacity of wildlife to survive if given only a moderate improvement in their environment.

Unlike air and water pollution, the tipping of mining and industrial refuse and the use of fly-ash and clinker as railway ballast may produce conditions which actually favour some of our more unusual wild plants. The lesser broomrape, for example, is encountered by the side of railway lines in Nottingham, and in one location yellow-wort flourishes on colliery spoil.

Disturbed habitats are often associated with urban decline. They include demolition sites and derelict land, old railway lines and canals. Yet surprisingly, these areas often support an abundant wildlife, including native and alien flowering plants which, during the summer months, provide a striking patch of colour within the heart of the City. Plants of waste places are referred to as ruderals; all produce abundant seed, which makes them particularly successful in the urban environment, where newly derelict ground is constantly available for colonisation. Many ruderals were formerly of limited distribution: rose-bay willow-herb was a rare plant in Britain until the mid-19th century, but it is now one of the most common urban species, which can be found growing on a large number of sites in Nottingham. Other plants may owe their abundance to the expansion of the railway network in the last century. Oxford ragwort, a frequent yellow-flowered composite of derelict sites, which is native to the island of Sicily, 'escaped' from Oxford botanic gardens at the start of this century, and its wind blown seeds were dispersed along railway lines, aided by the draught of the trains. It now occurs throughout much of Britain on railway ballast and rubble which are similar in composition to the dry, volcanic soils on the slopes of Mount Etna, whence this plant originated. Another successful pioneer plant of derelict land which grows on volcanic soils in its native, east Asian home, is the Japanese knotweed. This plant has spread rapidly following introduction into Britain and is now rampant on many urban sites, where it forms large bushes which shade out other plants. As a result of its invasive nature it is now an offence under the Wildlife and Countryside Act 1981 to introduce this plant into the wild.

Railway marshalling yards, embankments and tracks (both used and disused) are some of the more interesting disturbed habitats in Nottinghamshire. Here commonplace weeds grow beside introduced (alien) species, from as far away as North America and Asia; together they form colourful pioneer communities on the beds of clinker and cinder. Annual and biennial plants are abundant: scentless mayweed, Oxford ragwort, common poppy, yellow toadflax, coltsfoot and common melilot grow with the small yellow-flowered crucifers hedge mustard and wall rocket, which also have a preference for dry, warm soils, reflecting their origins in southern Europe. Other plants have come from further afield: Canadian fleabane and common evening primrose are North American species. These brightly-flowered ruderals form a mosaic with slender, fine-leaved grasses including rat's tail fescue and silver hair-grass. In late summer, the yellow swathes of these grasses outside Nottingham Midland Station are reminiscent of a miniature prairie. You can even find several prairie plants growing there, which have escaped from urban gardens, namely Michaelmas daisy and golden rod.

On disused railway lines in Nottingham other plants prosper which are of more limited distribution in the rest of the county. Fennel, for example, grows in abundance at Basford Junction and on other City centre sites, yet it is rare in the rest of the county.

On railway tracks that have been disused for a long time, the weed communities have been replaced by taller grasses and herbs. Pink and purple swathes of rose-bay willowherb, thistle and teasel replace the predominantly yellow- and white-flowered pioneer communities. Eventually scrub (usually of hawthorn, elder and buddleia) will invade. In Nottingham City centre, the steep, cliff-like sides of the Victoria Hole (all that remains of the former Victoria railway station) are covered with buddleia, but, on the floor of the 'Hole', the very alkaline nature of the old railway ballast is limiting scrub invasion. A later stage in this succession can be observed along Bulwell Forest Railway, a disused line in the north of the City. Here, oak-hawthorn scrub has established and, in the autumn months, woodland toadstools appear, including several edible species such as the miller, saffron milk cap, bare-toothed russula and, on the stems of elder, the liver-brown jew's ear.

The animal life of railway lines is equally varied. Butterflies are attracted by the presence of nectar-bearing flowers and larval food-plants on which eggs may be laid. Although various white butterflies are particularly common, more colourful species include the small copper, whose larvae feed on docks and sorrels, and large and small skippers, which lay their eggs on various grasses, whilst buddleia bushes attract small tortoiseshells, peacocks and red admirals. Grassy banks, especially south-facing ones, provide an ideal habitat for sun-loving grasshoppers, and flowering stands of willowherb and thistle attract bees and hoverflies, so that, on a warm, summer's day, these sites are literally humming with wildlife. Mammals, although less obvious, are also present. Under thickets of bramble and dog rose, alongside both used and disused railway lines, many foxes have their earths. Throughout the City centre they are able to raise their cubs largely undisturbed, except for the occasional passing train. At night they forage for food along the railway lines, in rubbish dumps and household dustbins. To the fox, the built environment now offers a more secure habitat than that of his country cousin.

In the longer grass of the railway embankment live small mammals—voles, mice and shrews—which, as well as providing furry snacks for the foxes, are also hunted by kestrels. This bird may be sighted in Nottingham, and appears to have adapted well to the urban environment, nesting in and on buildings within the City centre.

One of the largest areas of disturbed, derelict land in Nottingham lies on the site of the former Wilford Power Station. On varied industrial wastes—notably spent fuel ash from the power station—an extensive area of grassland has developed. On this large City-centre wasteland fennel is abundant, and amongst a variety of grass species grows the attractive pink-flowered common centaury, which belongs to the gentian family. These grasslands are also home to a family of partridges, a bird which is decreasing in rural areas owing to agricultural intensification, and in the autumn flocks of goldfinches strip the seed from teasels and thistles. As with the disused railway lines in the City, there is no formal management of this area. Many of the older industrial sites in Nottingham are, or have been, cleared and, as industrial estates begin to prosper, plans for urban or industrial development of those remaining may be put into effect.

Although ruderal communities are considered to be the only truly spontaneous vegetation of urban areas, other plant communities are also present, and frequently provide large areas of open green space within the City environment. The majority of these are well-managed ornamental gardens or recreation grounds, exhibiting low botanical diversity. Amenity grassland is the commonest type of open space within the towns of Nottinghamshire; this comprises parks and playing fields and in most cases rightly deserves the epithet 'urban savannah' comprising, as it does, large expanses of mown grassland with occasional ornamental trees. These have a low wildlife interest—the large open spaces provide little cover—although shrubberies may serve as nesting sites for blackbirds and song thrushes. Ornamental park lakes, for example University Park lake in Nottingham may attract mallard and moorhen, but they usually have a limited vegetation, particularly if they are concrete-lined or used intensively for recreation. Parks are important to local communities and often provide the only open spaces in the built environment. As a result of sympathetic planning and planting, many could be made more attractive to wildlife, and at the same time given a more pleasant, natural appearance.

Cemeteries, on the other hand, can be hospitable to wildlife, particularly if sections are left unmown until late in the season, allowing flowers to set seed. If managed correctly, cemeteries are far from dead places. The General Cemetery in Nottingham, for example, contains a variety of mature trees and shrubs, which provide nesting and roosting sites for songbirds (robins, blackbirds and wrens). Amongst the moss-covered gravestones grow oat grass, cocksfoot grass, Yorkshire fog, ox-eye daisies and cow parsley, and the older memorials are smothered with tangled masses of ivy and bindweed.

Nottingham also contains pockets of relict encapsulated countryside. These patches of pre-urban vegetation include grasslands, woodlands and wetlands. The grasslands usually form commons and parklands that have never been cultivated to any great extent or enclosed, although they are rarely areas of wilderness and usually have incorporated into them recreational facilities (golf courses, football pitches etc). In Wollaton Park, areas of old grassland are indicated by the presence of the fine-leaved crested dog's-tail grass and small flowering-plants, including harebell. The Park also contains an interesting area of damp alder and willow in Thompson's Wood and is home to several badgers, which occasionally visit the gardens of nearby houses during nocturnal forays in search of earthworms, insects or household scraps.

Bulwell Park is on the northern outskirts of Nottingham and here a major interest lies in an area of relict species-rich grassland. The underlying geology is Magnesian Limestone, and the plants are typical of calcareous grassland. Sweet vernal grass and the attractive quaking grass grow with common restharrow and yellow rattle, whose roots are semi-parasitic on those of the grasses. This small relict of the former countryside now lies between football pitches, yet it is as diverse as many other old grasslands on the limestone belt further north in the county. Hopefully its location in a park will ensure its survival since, in contrast to rural grasslands, it is unlikely to be threatened by agricultural 'improvement'.

Nottingham also contains several small patches of acidic grassland on outcrops of Sherwood Sandstone. Sunrise Hill, Bestwood Park is a designated conservation area and, although only 1.5 hectares (3.7 acres), it supports grasses which are characteristic of dry, sandy soils, for example red fescue, common bent-grass, wavy-hair grass and barren fescue. The bird life of this site is not varied, probably owing to the lack of suitable cover, but there are abundant common field grasshoppers on the dry grassy slopes. With advice and help from Nottingham Urban Wildlife Scheme the ornithological interest of this site will soon be increased, by planting native trees and shrubs.

Urban woodlands in Nottinghamshire range from remnants of ancient woodland, such as Broxtowe Wood and Seller's Wood on the north-western boundary of the City, to secondary plantation woodlands and smaller patches of planted or spontaneous scrub on road and railway verges and alongside canals. The older woodland sites pre-date urbanisation and are similar to the larger woodlands in the rural sections of the county, although the tree cover is sparser, and ground flora less diverse as a result of trampling, pollution and vandalism.

Harrisons Plantation, in its multifunctional use, is characteristic of many urban woodlands. It provides open space amidst suburban housing; it is walked by local residents; contains a pond used by a fishing club and an unofficial BMX track created by local children. The site is adjacent to Martin's Pond which is managed by Nottinghamshire Trust for Nature Conservation, and in the low-lying sections of the wood close to this pond grow alders and willows, principally crack willow, which may formerly have been planted to provide a source of wood for local craftsmen. The canopy of the drier areas is dominated by sycamore with a degraded, species-poor herb-layer of brambles, goosegrass and nettles. In the vicinity of the cycle track, where the ground is compacted, the ground flora is completely destroyed, but in less disturbed parts of the wood a few plants grow which are unusual within the urban environment, including the broad-leaved helleborine. The fish pond and the proximity to Martin's Pond have increased the ornithological interest of this site and, in addition to woodland birds (such as wren, nuthatch, tree creeper and great spotted woodpecker), occasional kingfishers visit, and herons use some of the larger trees as roosting sites. Biologists from the Nottingham Urban Wildlife Scheme have formulated a comprehensive management plan for this woodland. The principal aim is to increase the diversity of native species and habitats by selective removal of sycamore, and replanting with native hardwoods (oak, ash, alder, willow). An important aspect of this work, as with any successful urban environmental improvement scheme, is the support of local residents.

Thompson's Wood in Wollaton Park contains wooded marshland that has developed around an outflow stream from the adjacent ornamental lake. Willow and alder are the dominant trees, but in the drier sections of the wood, non-native and ornamental species such as sycamore and horse chestnut have been planted, and the ground flora in these areas is heavily grazed by the Park's resident red deer herd. The damper sections, however, are less disturbed, and support a diverse ground flora, which includes several noteworthy marshland species. Wood club-rush forms dense stands and other plants, which are unusual if not rare in an urban situation, include false fox-sedge, the pink-flowered ragged robin and common skull-cap, which has small trumpet-shaped blue-violet flowers.

By contrast, Alexandrina Plantation is an area of dry oak woodland and grassland, developed on acidic sandy soils overlying Sherwood Sandstone. A number of sandstone exposures occur, from the top of which fine views can be obtained over the City. The surrounding slopes are covered with low-growing pedunculate oak and silver birch woodland, and the ground flora contains foxglove and wood sage, which are characteristic plants of woodlands on acidic or basic soils. Where the canopy is more open, broom and bracken dominate.

Water-meadows and wetlands are rare in urban areas, the majority having been drained and reclaimed. As a result, plants and animals which have a preference for wet habitats, in particular reptiles and amphibians, are infrequently encountered. Nottingham, however, is particularly fortunate in containing several excellent remnant wetland sites along the valleys of the Rivers Trent and Leen, which support a varied wildlife, including common frog, common toad and possibly even adder. This venomous reptile, Britain's only poisonous snake, is capable of inflicting a painful bite on human victims, but the consequences are, fortunately, rarely fatal. Adders are rare in Nottinghamshire and their presence on an urban site gives added conservation value.

Moorbridge Pond is perhaps the foremost wetland site in Nottingham. It is situated around freshwater springs and is the last remnant of Bulwell Bogs which, in the past, covered large areas beside the banks of the River Leen. In the earlier part of this century the bogs were used as a bathing place by local inhabitants, but since then most of the water has been culverted for industrial use. The small site that remains contains a varied flora which includes plants of open, shallow water, low marshland vegetation and tall stands of sedge, reed-grass and reedmace. Four species of horsetail occur: water horsetail and the smaller marsh horsetail can be found in the marsh, whilst wood horsetail and common horsetail grow on the drier margins. Other wetland plants include wild angelica, water mint and water-cress, and floating on the surface of the water there are tiny fronds of common and ivy duckweed. The marsh is also home to a large number of frogs, toads and water voles, plus a less common inhabitant of urban sites, the common lizard.

The tall stands of reeds and sedges attract reed buntings and reed warblers, whilst overhead swifts and house martins swoop in search of flying insects. Moorbridge Pond is currently being managed by the Nottingham Urban Wildlife Scheme to realise its full potential for wildlife; young trees and shrubs have been planted around the margins and the area of open water has been increased to diversify the wetland habitat. Within a few weeks of this latter work being completed, snipe, heron and teal were observed. Future plans include construction of a bird-watching hide, which will add greatly to this site's value.

By contrast to Moorbridge Pond, Martin's Pond in Wollaton is largely artificial, urban wetland which may originally have been created as a medieval fish pond. Today, Martin's Pond serves as an informal recreation area for local residents, fishermen and naturalists. It has been designated a Local Nature Reserve by Nottinghamshire County Council and is adjacent to Harrison's Plantation. The vegetation is of interest within the urban environment, both because of its diversity and the presence of several noteworthy species. Large stands of lesser reedmace surround the pond, forming dense mats. This is a local plant in the British Isles, its close relative the great reedmace being more commonly encountered. Other marshland plants include ragged robin, and several plants with less attractive flowers, such as marsh arrow-grass and remote-flowered sedge. The pond is an important site within the City for birds, and provides food for migratory waders and wildfowl, as well as suitable habitats for woodland species in the scrub and trees around the water's edge. Although breeding success is limited by human disturbance, at least 20 species annually raise young at the site, including little grebe, great crested grebe and sedge warbler. Pochard and tufted duck are winter visitors, whilst in summer reed warblers and willow warblers take up residence. On a summer's night, bats can be sighted sweeping across the pond and adjoining woodland in search of insects; pipistrelle, long-eared and the larger noctule bats have been recorded. The pond itself is stocked with various coarse fish, but also contains crested and smooth newts.

Finally, perhaps the most important oasis for wildlife in the built environment is in our own back garden. Gardens are as varied as their owners, and range from well-manicured lawns to more disorderly jungles, in which a wealth of wildlife makes its home. Some large gardens are mini-nature reserves in their own right, with ponds full of frog spawn and resident hedgehogs. But even a tiny garden can be organised in such a way that it attracts a variety of wild visitors, as long as the bare essentials are provided—food, water and shelter. Bird tables and nut baskets bring greenfinches, blue and great tits into the garden where they show off their acrobatic skills to the less agile house sparrows. Butterfly visitors can be encouraged by growing plants with nectar-rich flowers. The large pink flowers of the ice-plant will draw tortoiseshell and peacock butterflies into the herbaceous border, whilst, at night, nicotinias and night-scented stocks will be visited by moths. A simple pile of old logs can house dozens of beetles, spiders and millipedes which, in their turn, attract familiar insectivorous garden birds such as the robin. Ponds are another important diversification of the garden environment, without which the frog population of Nottinghamshire would be seriously diminished as a result of the decline in suitable wetland breeding sites in the countryside. Even in our own homes we may, however unwittingly, play host to wild creatures. Bats have taken up residence in roof spaces on new housing estates; house martins build their nests under the eaves and, given half a chance, house mice will make short work of stored apples or jam. In 1986 an ordinary house in Nottingham provided a new record for the county, when a single serotine bat was found by a man working on the roof.

A substantial proportion of the City of Nottingham is composed of gardens and allotments. The full value for wildlife remains, as yet, unknown. But even without a systematic survey, it is clear that the gardens and their owners provide an important urban wildlife refuge.

Improvement and protection of wild spaces within the urban environment are the broad aims of the Nottingham Urban Wildlife Scheme and already, with the co-operation of the Nottingham

City Council, the scheme has achieved a great deal. One of the latest initiatives has been the creation in 1987 of what is probably Britain's first 'up in the air' urban nature reserve, located on Collins Street viaduct behind the Broadmarsh shopping centre. Work is already in hand to create a colourful wild flower nursery on this section of disused railway line and, although inaccessible to the general public, the results will be visible from surrounding roads and buildings.

When considered together, these old railway lines, plus the roadside verges and canals, form important green corridors along which wildlife can move, largely unhindered, into the heart of the City. Foxes have migrated into town along the railway lines, whilst moorhens, coots, mute swans and kingfishers have found their way into the City centre *via* canal or river. In Nottingham, many of these corridors link up with known sites of wildlife interest, to form a green network which supports a surprising variety of wildlife. Superimpose on this network the pattern of urban gardens and allotments and it becomes apparent that the City is an important natural resource for wildlife.

Improvements in the urban environment affect plants, animals and people alike. Cities become pleasanter places in which to live, work and spend one's leisure time, and children and adults can study nature close at hand rather than only on occasional trips to the countryside. These social benefits go hand in hand with urban nature conservation.

This chapter has concentrated on the City of Nottingham, partly because it has been closely studied in recent years, but also because it is, arguably, the most 'urban' of all of Nottinghamshire's urban centres. However, the same surprising richness of wildlife can be found elsewhere in the county: in the gardens of Worksop, in the quiet corners of Southwell, across the roofs and ledges of Sutton in Ashfield and in all the other urban nooks and crannies of the county's towns. The job of the nature conservation movement is to encourage it as much as possible, so that everyone can enjoy wildlife where they live.

Some of the birds of Nottingham look down upon the Council House. (KM)

ABOVE LEFT: Wall brown butterflies (M&DG) and RIGHT: large skippers (M&DG) add to the diversity of the county's flower meadow nature reserves. CENTRE LEFT: The six-spot burnet is another source of colour in the county's meadows. (M&DG) RIGHT: The painted lady is one of the butterflies to frequent Bestwood Country Park. (DW) BELOW: Safe forever. An ancient coppiced woodland in Nottinghamshire, bright with wood anemones and primroses, is one of the great symbols and success stories of the conservation movement. (M&DG)

PLATE V

ABOVE: Wildlife and industry are never far apart in Nottinghamshire. Beyond the cowslips of Ashton's Meadow nature reserve loom the towers of a Trentside power station. (M&DG) LEFT: Lady's smock, sometimes called cuckoo flower. (M&DG) RIGHT: Martin's Pond, an important urban wetland in Nottingham, is home to crested newts. (DW)

PLATE VI

ABOVE: Coltsfoot helps to brighten up both used and disused railway lines. (DW) LEFT: Peacocks (MDG), CENTRE: red admirals (MDG) and RIGHT: small tortoiseshells (HM) are attracted by buddleia bushes along railway lines.

ABOVE LEFT: A dramatic silhouette of a kestrel over urban wasteland. (M&DG) RIGHT: Wren's nest in the General Cemetery, Nottingham. (JW) BELOW LEFT: A headstone in nature's grip, General Cemetery, Nottingham. (SP) RIGHT: The broad leaved helleborine, found in Harrison's Plantation, is an unusual plant for an urban environment. (RHH)

ABOVE LEFT: Foxgloves grow in Alexandrina Plantation. (RHH)
RIGHT: A common toad turns its back on the camera to show off its warty
skin texture. (AG) BELOW LEFT: Mating common toads. (DW) RIGHT:
Common frogs are increasingly relying on garden ponds as suitable wetland
habitat in the countryside declines. (DSm)

LEFT: Great tits come to garden bird tables to supplement their diet in winter. (JW) RIGHT: The first serotine bat recorded in the county — found in a house in Nottingham 1986. (DW) BELOW: A mute swan dozes by a stretch of canal, (M&DG) and OPPOSITE ABOVE: others nest in the suburbs — West Bridgford, Nottingham. (SM) BELOW: Martin's Pond. (SM)

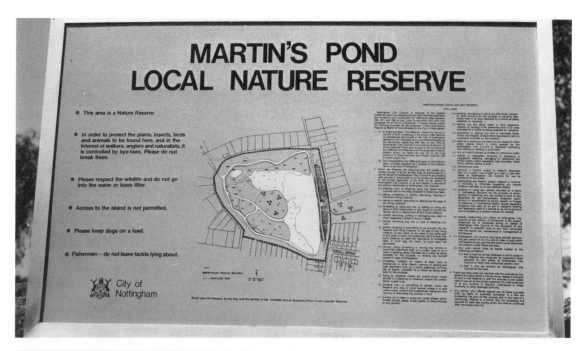

ABOVE: Local Nature Reserves are subject to many protective bye-laws. (HM) BELOW: View over the City from Alexandrina Plantation. Sherwood Sandstone outcrop in foreground. (SP)

ABOVE: Pedestrians stroll below Collins Street Viaduct, unaware of the wildlife interest above their heads. (SM) BELOW: Part of an abandoned railway line, it must be one of the most unusual wildlife sites in the country. (SM)

An aerial photograph shows the disused gravel workings which now form the basis for Colwick Country Park. The River Trent flows past to the south of the Park. (NCC)

Industry and its Impact

(KM)

Since earliest times the hand of man has been an important factor influencing habitat change and wildlife in our county. The development of the urban-industrial base of the county in the last century and its expansion in the present century has arguably made the human factor of supreme importance.

The western third of the county has become a loosely structured conurbation where most of the county's one million population is concentrated. Here urban and urban fringe land uses impose themselves on the environment, from Nottingham and Beeston in the south, through the Erewash Valley towns, to Mansfield and Worksop in the north.

Nottinghamshire however, is a county where industrialisation extends well beyond the main built-up areas. This results from the prominence of extractive industries in the county economy, coal, sand and gravel being the main ones, supplemented by gypsum, brick and fire clays, moulding sands, oil, magnesian limestone and others. Interconnecting the mines and quarries with the urban areas have developed networks of canals, mineral railways and, of course, roads. Moreover the coal industry attracted other manufacturing, which used coal as a vital energy source and later led to the development along the Trent valley of the country's biggest concentration of coal-fired electricity power stations.

Whilst it may not be far from the truth to say that there are few places in Nottinghamshire where a coal mine, sand and gravel quarry or other industrial installation is out of sight, it should by no means be thought that the interest of our county to the naturalist is inevitably diminished. Some of our most valued wildlife habitats have resulted directly from industrialisation. Furthermore some of the most exciting challenges for conservation lie in the management of post-industrial sites of which many have already been designated as nature reserves.

The origins of one of the key extractive industries of the county can be traced back to the Ice Ages. Glacial outwash gravels and pebbles from the Triassic beds were subsequently re-sorted by the great post-glacial rivers to form the terrace gravels of the Trent and Idle Valleys. They are among the most important reserves of construction aggregate in the country, producing over three million tons per annum. Major gravel workings are located at Attenborough, Colwick, Holme Pierrepont, Gunthorpe, Hoveringham, Muskham, Collingham, Besthorpe and Girton in the Trent valley, and in the Lound and Misson areas of the Idle valley. They have proved to be of considerable palaeontological as well as ecological interest, with the unearthing of mammoth teeth and tusks amongst other animal remains, and human implements dating back to the Stone Age.

105

Most of the workings are below the water table and are either worked as wet pits or are flooded after working and the cessation of pumping. The water-filled lagoons form a chain at irregular intervals down the whole of the Trent Valley, and as such are a strategically important flyway for wildfowl and passage waders, gulls and terns. Most of the wintering wildfowl in the county concentrate on the gravel pits, with typical peaks of over 5,000 mallard, over 1,000 each of teal, tufted duck and wigeon, over 300 great crested grebes, between 2/300 shoveler, over 100 goldeneye and smaller numbers of other ducks, geese and swans. Peaks occur at different times: shovelers in August and September, diving ducks in January and February and great crested grebes in March. Cold spells often make gravel pits the haunts of rare slavonian and black-necked grebes, divers, sawbills (smew, goosander and red-breasted merganser) and sea ducks. Spring and autumn migration bring a wide variety of waders, gulls and terns, whilst late autumn gales can often cause pelagic species of seabirds to be blown inland to these sites. It is not infrequent to have to take manx shearwaters and other petrels to the coast for release after convalescence.

The longer established workings, such as Attenborough, which was begun in the 1920s, represent the most mature colonisation and most diverse communities of plants and animals. Attenborough was the county's first nature reserve and other gravel pits subsequently designated as reserves are at Holme Pierrepont, Besthorpe and Daneshill. Often however, gravel workings produce only temporary habitats which, when working has ceased, are used for tipping, and restored to agriculture or alternatively developed for recreation, when wildlife has to share space with fishermen, as at Colwick Country Park, or water sportsmen, as at the Holme Pierrepont National Watersports Centre. Joint use with recreation can sometimes still sustain the wildlife interest of these watery places, but the most valued sites warrant retention for nature alone. Unfortunately many fine areas are lost entirely, restoration to agriculture having been so fiercely upheld by the farming and land owning lobby. Only the accident of inadequate filling materials has slowed down the restoration machine, and conservationists must argue their case for nature reserves more vehemently.

Sand and gravel workings do not constitute a single uniform habitat but a complex of varied habitats: the freshwater lagoons of varying depths; the exposed sand faces and gravel surfaces of new workings; the rough grasslands which surround and inter-penetrate the pits, some on disturbed ground with rank herbaceous vegetation; the unworked and fringing marshes and reed fens; areas of willow scrub often representing ancient willow holts or their newly colonised extensions; small areas of woodland and thorn scrub on islands in the pits; and, where there are gravel processing plants, deltaic deposits of sand and silt formed by workings and displaying various stages of plant succession. Abandoned sand faces on the edge of gravel pits attract breeding sand martins, sometimes in large, densely-packed colonies. Their arrival from March and more numerously in April has been one of the ornithological highlights of the gravel pit year. The sound of massed flights of twittering sand martins at the height of the breeding season may be accompanied by the sight of the irridescent blue flash of a kingfisher, which commonly uses similar nest sites. Basal surfaces and spits of gravel are the classic habitat for the dapper little ringed plover which, more than any other bird, is dependent on gravel workings. Its spread nationally and locally has mirrored the expansion of the sand and gravel industry. During the migration period it is accompanied by other species of plovers and sandpipers and at some gravel pits, especially in the north of the county, it has been joined as a breeding species by the closely similar but orange-legged ringed plover and by the oystercatcher. These habitats are short-lived except where there is positive management of unstable sand faces, or to suppress the colonisation of exposed gravel beds by willow seedlings and ruderal plants such as docks. Exposed gravel and clay surfaces are anyway soon flooded when working has ceased. It tends therefore to be the newer workings where these habitats are concentrated.

The flooded pits are not initially rich in plant or invertebrate life, but even at this stage represent safe roost sites for wildfowl and gulls. One of the largest gull roosts in the county has been at Hoveringham. The shallow fringes of the lagoons soon begin to be colonised by Norfolk reed, common reedmace with its poker-like seed head, dense mats of reed sweetgrass, water plantain, horsetails, branched bur-reed, and various rushes and sedges such as pond sedge, false fox sedge, and the graceful pendulous sedge. True aquatic plants also colonise, including various waterweeds, pondweeds, duckweeds and some of the beautiful water milfoils. The vegetal detritus from other bankside plants adds to the humus content of the pits. The development of this plant colonisation attracts plant-feeding waterfowl such as dabbling ducks (mallard and teal), wigeon, moorhen and coot, mute swans and Canada geese, the last numbering in their hundreds in post-breeding flocks at Attenborough and Hoveringham.

Water scorpion.   Great diving beetle.   Great diving beetle larva.

Swan mussel.   Ramshorn snail.   Freshwater shrimp.

Some of the underwater creatures found in flooded gravel pits, (not drawn to scale). (WE)

Plant colonisation of the pits also creates the conditions for an increasing richness of invertebrates and fish. On the surface, in sheltered bays, one will see water boatmen, pond skaters and water measurers. At the bottom, in shallow waters, water shrimps are numerous and may be accompanied by water scorpions, freshwater sponges on submerged logs and stones and the aquatic larvae of insects such as midges, caddis flies, alder fly, dragonflies, and damselflies. Deeper waters are the abode of ramshorn and other pond snails, spire shells, swan and zebra mussels. Many other aquatic invertebrates swell the diversity and numbers and a particularly fine 38 mm (inch and a half) long species of some sites is the great diving beetle. One sometimes forgets that this species can fly until one finds it on a warm summer evening in a mist net erected to catch birds for ringing. At Attenborough the great diving beetle (*Dytiscus marginalis*) is accompanied by its close fenland relative, *Dytiscus circumcinctus*. Aquatic invertebrates are taken by shovelers, which filter out the small surface species, and by diving ducks which exploit the deeper waters for snails and mussels.

Vegetated islands in the lagoons shelter breeding and loafing wildfowl, whilst bare, low islands are valued nest sites for common terns at a number of pits. Unfortunately these islands are susceptible to flooding, and the population of common terns at Attenborough has been helped to expand by the provision of an artificial nest platform. Black terns attempted to nest at Attenborough in the 1970s but are most commonly seen on migration associated with easterly winds, as they fly gracefully low across the water, dipping at the surface for their mainly insect diet. Black-headed gulls breed on islands at some of the northern and eastern gravel pits, but predation by rats, foxes, the larger gulls and miscreant humans can be high.

The variety of fish in a gravel pit can be considerable, though the dominant species are usually roach, bream, tench, carp and pike. Both populations and size can be large in nutritious waters, making them attractive to fish-eating birds and fishermen respectively. Amongst the former, the gravel pits hold important populations of great crested grebes, whose springtime display is a fascinating spectacle, with the mutual shaking of heads adorned by orange tippets, fish and weed presentation ceremonies and occasionally the climactic 'cat' and 'penguin' displays. Attenborough Nature Reserve holds one of the largest breeding populations in the Midlands of this once much-slaughtered species. Grey herons, sentinels of many a shallow water's edge, are also common fishermen and breed on and adjacent to at least three gravel pits. Sawbill ducks and, less often, divers join them fishing in winter. Great northern and black-throated divers seem especially attracted to the Colwick-Holme Pierrepont complex, perhaps attracted by trout-stocked waters! Meanwhile Attenborough holds a growing winter population of cormorants. Over 100 have been counted at the roost though, fortunately for our good relations with the fishermen, they feed elsewhere.

In some gravel workings, the aquatic habitats are complemented only by surrounding grassland and rough herbage. This is substantially true of the Girton, Muskham and Hoveringham complexes. Other workings contain grassland habitats on varying scales amongst their more diverse habitat structure.

This combination of ponds and grassland is particularly attractive to grazing waterfowl, such as wigeon and geese, and where shallow silt deposits are also present, waders are attracted in good numbers, preferring the security of open habitats to the closed ones where woodland and scrub surround the margins of the pits.

Grassland disturbed by workings contains a rich growth of common field weeds and ruderal herbs. The particular species will vary from site to site, depending on soil nutrients, alkalinity and drainage. One site may be white over with mayweed whilst another is ablaze with poppies, or yellow with St John's worts and tansy, or green with docks, goosefoots and oraches. Wetter sites may have species such as trifid bur-marigold, whilst free draining sands contain toadflax, or more rarely, birdsfoot and haresfoot clover. The ranker vegetation may be dominated by nettle, marsh and spear thistle, with persicaria, great burnet, and the poisonous hemlock. Nutrient-poor areas are where one will find various vetches and cinquefoils. Centaury, red bartsia and crow garlic are recorded where the soil is fairly alkaline, whilst more acid conditions favour harebell and sheep's sorrel on the higher terraces.

These grasslands are the domain of meadow butterflies (meadow brown, wall brown, small tortoiseshell, common blue, small copper and occasionally ringlet) and other insects in profusion, including many beautiful beetles and plant bugs. They can also hold good populations of voles, shrews and mice, which no doubt emphasise their attraction to hovering kestrels and also quartering short-eared owls in winter. The dominant passerine birds of the shorter grassland are skylark, meadow pipit, yellow wagtail and that most under-rated wader, the lapwing. Taller marshy grasslands hold mainly the voluble sedge warbler (and sometimes the reeling grasshopper warbler), the unmusical reed bunting, its cousin the yellowhammer and flocks of finches, including red and yellow bedecked charms of goldfinches. This latter habitat is also the place to look for the jaunty whinchat, whilst wheatears on passage will be found on the short grassland.

Most gravel workings contain some fringing marsh. This is only extensive when it pre-dates the workings or when the banks are unusually gently shelved. Attenborough contains some fine marsh and fen habitat whilst Daneshill has some of the few acid bogs in the county, with their distinctive sphagnum mosses and fungi. Typical plants of the fens and marshes include water dock, fool's watercress, fine-leaved and tubular water dropwort, celery-leaved crowfoot, meadowsweet, purple loosestrife, great willow herb, water forget-me-not, water mint, water figwort, water plantain, flowering rush and yellow iris. Both greater and lesser reed-mace occur and of course many reeds, rushes and sedges. The list could be seemingly endless, and even more important is the apparently infinitely variable mixes of species which occur. An exception is where the introduced Himalayan balsam has taken over with its rapid growth rate, to produce a late-season flush of exotic pink, mauve or purple flowers with explosive seeds and heavy odours.

These marshes contain shallow pools which are rich locations for dragonflies and amphibians. The brown hawker is the typical dragonfly easily distinguished by its brown wings. It is joined by the smaller common darter later in the season. At Attenborough and some other sites the beautiful southern and migrant hawkers can also be added, together with the scarce and dazzling four-spotted chaser. Typical damselflies are the common azure, the blue-tailed (with all its female colour forms), the large red, the common blue (less common in fact than the superficially similar azure) and the beautiful and large banded demoiselle (closer to flowing water). Perhaps a lucky person might see the emerald damselfly, but it must not be confused with the female of the previous species which is also an irridescent green.

Sedge warbler, reed warbler and reed bunting may dominate the breeding birds of the marsh. Moorhens are sometimes supplemented by water rails and rare crakes in winter. Cuckoos predate the reed warbler colonies. Large roosts of swallows and sand martins form at some marshes in autumn, and these may be replaced by reed buntings and pied-wagtails in winter. Winter has also been known to bring bearded tits and even bitterns with surprising regularity. Water voles, falsely maligned by the name 'rat', can usually be seen sitting chewing the emergent plants, whilst summer evenings bring bats to hawk the overflying insects. The main species of bat are the small pipistrelles, the rufous noctule, the long-eared bat and probably Daubenton's bat, which characteristically flies low over water. Earlier in the day, the swarms of midges round the marsh may have been the prey of other aerial aces, the swifts.

Fen develops progressively into willow carr and, later, alder. Some areas of willow represent residual parts of ancient 'holts' where the trees were coppiced for basket making, thatching and hurdles. Others are more recently colonised on gravel pits, a process which, in the case of willows and their windblown seeds, can be remarkably rapid. The Nottinghamshire Trust for Nature Conservation has instituted a programme of coppicing the young stands of willow on the Attenborough delta, and of pollarding some of the large old willows, thus re-introducing the traditional systems of managing willow. The older areas of willow may contain a greater variety of species and hybrids which are a challenge in identification even to the expert. Attenborough has 14 species, sub-species and recognised hybrids. Undisturbed areas are also locations for black poplars, ash, thornscrub, elder, buckthorn and other scrub species. Alder may progressively develop in the damper sites, fixing nitrogen through its root nodules in waterlogged soils, whilst the free-draining sands may have birch colonisation and are even suitable for the introduction of oak. Crack and white willow dominate the canopy layer, with common osier and sallow forming the main scrub layer. Their early spring catkins attract the first insects, and in turn the first chiffchaffs and willow warblers of the year.

Outwash deltas and disturbed ground with a high water table typically develop as mixed reed fen and willow carr. This regime is being deliberately sustained by management at the Attenborough reserve. The whole succession from uncolonised silt, through reed fen, to coppiced and mature willow and alder carr is displayed. Golden dock is a pioneer species whilst some of the typical flowering plants of the later succession are ragged robin, cuckoo flower, meadowsweet, purple loosestrife, centaury, skull-cap gypsywort, hemp agrimony, yellow flag and spotted orchid. The last makes a profuse show at the Skylark's Reserve, Holme Pierrepont, and is present at many other sites. Springtime generally makes a beautiful display, with orange-tip butterflies visiting the cuckoo flowers, and brimstone butterflies in the areas where its larval food plant, buckthorn, is present. Comma butterflies have also increased recently. Lunar hornet clearwing moths, though rarely seen in their brief flight, are evidenced by their larval holes in the coppiced stumps of osiers. Another interesting moth, near its northern limit, is the shuttle-shaped dart, the adult flying in marshy areas in late April and May. Poplar hawks are quite common, as are willow beauties, associated with their respective food plants. Later in the year, the typical fungi are shaggy and other inkcaps in profusion, with elder having the aptly named jew's ear fungus. Bryophytes have been less thoroughly studied but one square foot of old willow bark studied recently revealed six species of mosses, six species of lichens and three species of liverworts: a rich miniature garden.

Willows and reeds both attract a rich assortment of plant invertebrates, which are a valuable food source for warblers. Willow warblers, chiffchaffs, blackcaps and garden warblers prefer the willows, whilst reed warbler populations are highest where there is mixed reed and young willow. Tit populations are also high, especially where there are old willows with suitable nest holes. In these circumstances, both species of spotted woodpeckers may also be found, together with tawny owls and commoner woodland birds. Woodcock are common in those damp woods in winter, whilst the open fen edges have snipe and the smaller and scarcer jack snipe.

Gravel pits do indeed have such a richness of wildlife that nature lovers of all kinds find plenty to interest them. Managed as nature reserves, they are amongst the greatest treasures of our county and provide some recompense for the loss of once natural floodwaters, marshes and wet meadowlands, which stretched throughout the Trent Valley before the major flood protection and land drainage schemes of the post-war era. For a further example of post-industrial habitat we must again remind ourselves of the geology of the county, and return to the humid swamps of about 300 million years ago. These ever-changing swamps, with their fast-growing trees and ferns being hawked over by giant dragonflies, were eventually transformed into the invaluable fossil fuel of coal. The trees and plants of the Carboniferous period locked away the sun's energy in these remote times, and the bringing to the surface of this ancient store of energy has created over the last few hundred years the giant colliery workings and pit tips for which the county is so well known.

These dirt tips are a reflection of coal's importance in economic terms, and indeed much of the wealth of Britain was created by the use of coal to power industry. A fine example of this creation of wealth is the beautiful Elizabethan mansion of Wollaton Hall, with its magnificent deer park. Now housing Nottingham's Natural History Museum, it was built from the proceeds of the Old Wollaton pit and many old workings are still to be found in the Wollaton area.

Because of the nature of geology in Nottinghamshire, the coal seams are generally concealed deep below the earth's surface, sloping from west to east and lying under the permo-triassic rocks which, in the south of the county, include the Bulwell Magnesian Limestone as well as the Sherwood Sandstone which outcrops to form the famous city landmark of Nottingham Castle Rock.

The depth of the coal seams requires deep shafts, and the digging of these and the underground tunnels for the extraction of the coal brings to the surface, as well as coal itself, great quantities of waste material in the form of rock and shale. For each ton of coal extracted there is approximately half a ton of waste to be tipped. With 20 working collieries in the county, Nottinghamshire is the largest coalfield in Britain, producing around 18.5 million tons of coal annually with the corresponding amount of waste material to be disposed of by surface tipping. Prior to nationalisation there was little preparation of the sites to be used for tipping. Often waste was tipped as it was extracted, onto existing top soil on the land around the colliery workings. The restoration of these sites has in the recent past been undertaken by local authorities with grant aid from central government. To cover the old spoil heaps, new soil has had to be found from many sources, including housing development sites and sugar beet factories, using the residue of soil washed from the sugar beet prior to processing. The prime aim is to return restored sites to agricultural, forestry or amenity purposes.

The mixture of local soil on these early tips would have an influence on the type of indigenous flora colonising their untreated fringes. In addition, many seeds are transported to these sites along with the imported soil. Some old tips are seeded with grass without the addition of top soil, the surface being scarified and, if required, a fertiliser applied before sowing. If trees are being planted, the surface of the tip is loosened by a heavy roter or a ridge and furrow surface is prepared.

Old dirt tips that have achieved a state of equilibrium, where combustion and erosion of the surface have ceased and native colonising plants have become established, are by far the most interesting types of habitat from the naturalist's view. Many such occur in association with the old collieries on the westernmost side of the county. Often the sites are havens for wildlife, colonising plants having in time attracted insects and other invertebrates to form part of the food chain. Moreover, the drainage lagoons, which are a necessary feature of the tip, attract amphibians, after they become stabilised by aquatic vegetation such as broad-leaved pondweed and, along the margins, by rushes and sedges.

Many of the early colonising plants are the showy members of the *compositae* family such as the ox-eye daisy, the early flowering coltsfoot, ragwort, dandelion as well as great and black knapweeds and goatsbeard. The wind-borne seeds of many of these plants provide rich pickings for small birds, especially the finches. Legumes such as birdsfoot trefoil and yellow melilots also occur and the ubiquitous teasel, another favourite food plant of the finches, finds a niche on the tips.

These invasive species are able to tolerate both acid and alkaline soil types thus taking advantage of the varying stages of pH (a measure of acidity/alkalinity) found on unrestored tips. Fresh discard when tipped is usually neutral or slightly alkaline. After some time, depending on various changes in the basic material and the effects of weathering, spoil may become increasingly acidic, with a consequent effect upon the flora, when the more acid-tolerant plants may occur such as gorse and broom.

Pit tips are not as stable as may appear in the short term, but any changes in the pH are slow, and therefore the effect of these changes on the flora is only perceived over fairly long periods.

A fine example of an untreated and naturally colonised tip is to be found at Bestwood Country Park north of Nottingham, where the top of the old tip has been left untreated and, apart from the old drainage system, unworked since tipping ceased. Biologists working in the park find this area of far greater interest than those sown with agricultural grasses, and more interesting even than some of the woodland areas of the park.

Almost as many invertebrates are found on the old tip as in the woodlands. Interestingly, the pill woodlouse, so called because of its habit of rolling into a pill shape when threatened, is found in calcareous areas. The harvestman, *Opilio saxataris,* occurs as does the small black garden ant

Lasius niger. Spiders are found and, unusually, a tiny uncommon species, *Milliana unerrans*, has been found recently. Among the many kinds of beetle to be found is the devil's coachhorse or cocktail beetle. Butterflies abound and those commonly seen include the red admiral, peacock, and painted lady, as well as the ubiquitous small tortoiseshell. The brown butterflies are represented by the meadow brown, small heath, wall and sometimes the dark brown ringlet. White and yellow butterflies, the pierids, are frequently to be found during the warmer spring and summer days, the commonest being the small and large whites which, although attractive, are not welcomed by the keen vegetable gardener. The green-veined white is also found along with the orange-tip and the earliest flying and most striking of the pierids, the brimstone. A flash of blue on a fine warm day reveals the male common blue butterfly, to which the rough hillsides created by the sloping tip approximate to its more usual downland habitat. The skippers are another group which find the pit tip habitat ideal, and representatives of this group, the hesperids, are the large and small skippers attracted by the profusion of flowers and also the grasses which provide food for the larval stage of this group of butterflies.

Many species of birds have been observed over the older pit tips. Some of the species seen over the Bestwood and Gedling tips are quite impressive. A sponsored bird watch at Gedling tip on a May Sunday in 1986 counted 61 species, including some interesting and unexpected examples such as wheatear, kingfisher and long-tailed tits. Most of the finches and several warblers including blackcaps and whitethroat, were also seen. Ground-nesting birds such as skylark and coveys of partridge, both our native grey and the introduced red-legged, are frequently seen on the pit tops, even those near urban areas such as Babbington.

A splendid example of the opportunities provided by the older pit tips for nesting birds occurred in 1973, when little ringed plovers successfully bred at Bestwood. Not surprisingly the hosts of small birds exploiting the feeding on these pit tips attracts the predators, and sparrowhawks and kestrels are frequently seen searching for prey. Kestrels actually nest within the colliery yard at Bestwood, using the old winding tower as a secure base to raise their young.

Mammals can also take advantage of the new opportunities afforded by the creation of pit waste. Often these areas offer a safer refuge than the surrounding farmland, especially for the brown hare and rabbit. Within a few months of the tipping of spoil from Cotgrave colliery, hares could be seen running over the lunar-like landscape of fresh spoil. As soon as vegetation appears whether naturally or sown by man, rodents such as the wood mouse or long-tailed field mouse invade the new horizons of space, where they are able to exploit the first crop of seeds and berries as they appear. House mice and short-tailed voles also make good use of the new food supply, the short-tailed vole especially liking the longer vegetation, where it can make its network of runways through the denser grasses and feed at the bases of the grass stems. The more agile bank vole appears when the scrub layer becomes established. This delightful animal is able to climb well, and soon benefits from the fruits and berries, as well as the small insects which form about a third of its diet.

Brown rats and house mice are common around buildings where man eats or stores food. They were extremely common when pit ponies were fed and housed underground. Descendants of these animals, although in fewer numbers, would soon find a niche on the pit tip when a colliery ceased production. They dig their tunnels into the less compacted materials on the pit tip, and are well able to survive on plant material and seeds as well as a wide range of invertebrates. Brown rats will also eat other small rodents such as the house mouse.

So far, no known records of harvest mice exist for pit tips in the county, but it can only be a matter of time before our smallest and probably most attractive rodent is found. Certainly all its requirements both for food and shelter exist on many older pit tips. Both pygmy and common shrews already occur on many tips, even on the restored tip at Cinderhill, where the local cats have been known to catch those vocal and highly territorial insectivores. Where there is standing water on tips such as Bestwood, it is likely that the larger water shrew may be found.

ABOVE LEFT: The kingfisher, found in several urban sites in Nottingham, is surely one of nature's most colourful creatures. (DS) RIGHT: Great spotted woodpeckers are visitors to Harrison's Plantation. (DS) BELOW LEFT: The ubiquitous blue tit — as much at home in a town garden as an ancient wood. (DS) RIGHT: Shorter grassland around gravel pits often holds populations of yellow wagtail. (DS)

PLATE VII

LEFT: The magnificent yellow flag — a flower of Attenborough nature reserve. (M&DG) CENTRE: The bee orchid (M&DG) and RIGHT: the green-winged orchid (M&DG) are among the many plants to flourish at BELOW: the Wilwell Farm Cutting nature reserve. (M&DG)

PLATE VIII

Several species of bats can be seen feeding over pit tips. Adjacent to Bestwood tip a colony of noctules is known to roost, and pipistrelles and brown long eared bats have been seen flittering over Babbington tip. Other as yet unidentified species have also been seen exploiting the abundant insect crop over a number of the county's pit tips.

Predators of these small mammals include foxes and kestrels, the latter regularly to be seen hovering, reminding us of their alternative name, windhover. Tawny and little owls also take their toll of the abundant small animal population as do the occasional stoat and the more frequently seen weasel. Feral cats, joined by their cosseted cousins, also take their share of the rodents and shrews, often killing the latter and leaving them because they are deterred by the musky scent glands.

Apart from the colliery tips, the other major habitats created by deep mining for coal are subsidence flashes, successive underground working of coal seams resulting in the lowering of the overlying strata and consequently the surface itself, in low lying areas, can subside below the water table to produce a 'flash'. Many such flashes are only transient features and have been drained in the course of river improvements and land drainage, or restored by tipping, or even destroyed in the process of opencast coal working. Two major flashes remain for the time being, in the Erewash valley at Brinsley and Aldercar, though these too are threatened by opencast mining proposals. The flashes and their environs are of interest for the plant life of both the aquatic and marginal habitats of the flash itself, and the wet meadows of the surrounding grassland. They also have a rich population of invertebrates. However it is the bird life of the flashes which is their main attraction. They are the main centres in the Erewash valley for wildfowl and also for passage waders. Whilst not holding the numbers attracted by the Trent valley, they have a rich diversity. Redshank and snipe inhabit the wet meadows and fringes. Teal are amongst the most numerous winter duck, and the flashes are the most reliable places to see, or more likely hear, water rails. The combination of all the wetland birds with those of adjoining farmland and woodland makes the flashes an interesting place for bird watching. At Aldercar Flash a colliery tip and subsidence flash exist side by side, such that there is the chance of seeing little ringed plovers breeding on the flanks of the tip and feeding on the flash. Collieries can therefore claim to have brought more than economic wealth to our county. Many of the places left in a so-called 'derelict' state after mining has stopped are well worth our closer attention and care.

Besides collieries and sand and gravel workings, other disused quarries have also been colonised by interesting communities of plants and animals, the particular make-up of which varies depending on geological and ground water conditions. A number of these are designated and managed as nature reserves, including Lady Lee Quarry near Worksop, Staunton Quarry near Newark, Wilford Clay Pit on the southern fringe of Nottingham and Stonepit Plantation near Strelley. Many of these combine geological with biological interest, aquatic and terrestrial communities and in some instances even calcicole (lime-loving) and calcifuge (lime-hating) plants, all within a small compass. Wilford Clay Pit is a fine example of one such small quarry. Enriched by alkaline ground water from Liassic Marls, it is colonised by a wondrous display of three species of orchids: centaury, yellow-wort, purging flax and other calcicoles, as well as fen species and colonists of disturbed ground normally associated with arable land. All this is within a few hectares, surrounded by industrial and residential developments. Lady Lee and Staunton are flooded limestone quarries of the Permian and Liassic series respectively.

Disused railways, of which the county has many hundred kilometres, likewise have been colonised by a vast majority of wildlife which otherwise would be scarce in a lowland county which has suffered extensive urban development, agricultural intensification, opencast coal working and other operations damaging to its ecological richness. Disused railways may be thought of as the linear equivalent to quarries and tips. As such they combine the value of semi-natural communities of plants and animals, with their value as existing or potential recreational footpaths and bridleways. Like the quarries, their particular wildlife interest varies with local geology and land use.

The Meden Trail reserve near Mansfield represents plant communities of the Magnesian Limestone with nettle-leaved and giant bellflower, ramsons, marjoram, basil, traveller's joy, mountain currant and other typical plants as well as areas of marsh, bird-rich ash woodland and a gorge with bryophytes and bat caves. Nearby Creswell Crags, a country park jointly managed by Nottinghamshire and Derbyshire County Councils, has similar interest and a renowned Palaeolithic and Neolithic history. The Clarborough Tunnel and Cutting reserve exhibits calcicole plant communities with pyramidal orchid, spiney restharrow, yellow-wort and other interesting plants, as well as a good variety of butterflies and other insects. Wilwell Farm Cutting reserve, south of Nottingham, has some similar calcicoles, four species of orchids including bee and green-winged, neutral grassland plants with adder's tongue fern and cypress spurge, small contrasting areas of acid bog and alkaline fen and mixed sallow, thorn and elder scrub. Its birds of note are whinchat and wintering owls. The reserves of Kimberley Cutting and Bentinck Banks bring us back to the Permian beds of the west of the county and a combined geological and botanical interest. Many more kilometres of disused railways have a recognised scientific interest and even those which are not so distinguished are treasured by local people as natural areas for enjoyment of amenity. Children use them for play in contact with nature and schools use them for educational purposes. Our disused railway network provides a fine cross-section of the county's natural history.

Reclamation of some areas has fragmented it, but the potential of the remainder as a trail network is gradually being recognised. The Farnsfield-Southwell Trail has already been established by the County Council. The west of the county has especially fine opportunities for an integrated system of trail lines. The County and District Councils are developing these in consultation with the Nottinghamshire Trust for Nature Conservation. They have rocky crags (in cuttings), acid grassland (on clinker and sands), alkaline grassland (on native limestone or imported chippings) and scrub woodland, the grasslands being rich in their butterfly populations and the scrub holding good numbers of warblers. Small mammals are common and even badger setts occur on some lines. Every kilometre has something of interest, damp shaded cuttings contrast with free-draining and exposed embankments, even north-facing slopes contrast with those facing sunny south. Some plants have an especial association with railways. Common and pale toadflax, Oxford ragwort, rose bay willow herb and everlasting pea are examples easily found. They have spread along the railway lines. Why not follow them?

Turning now to canals, their water levels were often maintained by feeder reservoirs. Such was the function of Moorgreen Reservoir in Broxtowe. It originally supplied the Nottingham Canal near where it joined the Erewash and Cromford Canals, and is itself fed by brooks draining through a dumble from the Felley Estate. It is surrounded by a mix of oak woods, dense sallows, white willows, birch, conifers, and marshland, as well as farmland and has water fennel and other pondweeds growing in its shallows. It holds good numbers of the commoner wintering duck and these can frequently be joined by scarcer varieties. Woodcock perform their roding flights in the vicinity and sparrowhawks are regular whilst, on a winter visit especially, the weir is always worth checking for grey wagtails. They sometimes stay to breed, making Moorgreen one of the few breeding sites in the county for a bird associated more typically with the faster flowing streams of the Derbyshire Peak and other upland areas.

Another body of water with industrial origins is the 28 hectare (70 acre) Kings Mill Reservoir alongside the A38 near Mansfield. It was a large 'mill-pond' supplying over 22,700 litres (5,000 gallons) of water per minute for the Kings Mill in the 19th century. It has attractive, predominantly semi-natural banks with a wide variety of trees, some grassland, much soft rush and areas of reed and reedmace. Like Moorgreen, it is a good haunt for waterfowl, notable

114

regulars amongst which are ruddy ducks. It also has a roost of mainly black-headed gulls and a varied if not numerous wader passage. Unfortunately it suffers considerable disturbance from water sports, having public access all round and a newly built by-pass on one side. Other mill ponds such as Pleasley are regrettably being lost as a result of the dewatering which mining subsidence causes.

We have concentrated on those post-industrial habitats which are most typical of our county. Many other treasured sites owe their origins to industry, and the process of creating new habitats never stops. We simply must ensure that the best from the past are safeguarded and that new opportunities are grasped imaginatively to create habitats from industrial wasteland. The changing attitudes of industrialists, mineral operators and public authorities hold out real hope. The county Trust is now widely consulted by those bodies for specialist advice on conservation and has secured leases, management agreements and licences on many sites as a result of good co-operation with industry. These sites should be the fore-runners of many more but, in a county so much of which is underlain by mineral reserves, the momentum must be maintained to turn the tide against the loss of wildlife.

Wood mice are some of our commonest mammals. (KM)

LEFT: A gravel pit willow bursts with seeds. (NL) RIGHT: A drake tufted duck shows off its tuft to perfection. (M&DG) BELOW: Gravel pits in Nottinghamshire hold important populations of great crested grebes. (JF)

ABOVE: The dapper little ringed plover has benefitted enormously from the habitat provided by the county's gravel pits. (JF) LEFT: Plants such as the pendulous sedge eventually colonise the fringes of the lagoons formed by gravel workings. (RHH) RIGHT: An Attenborough cormorant silhouetted against the sky. (AG)

117

ABOVE: The mallard (duck and drake seen here) is probably the most familiar of all our ducks. (M&DG) LEFT: Old willows which may be found around gravel pits attract birds such as the great spotted woodpecker on the look out for the nest hole. (DS) RIGHT: Swallows are familiar birds hawking for insects over the water, before returning to their hungry youngsters, safely tucked away in farm outbuildings or similar sites. (JF)

118

ABOVE: The beautiful but sadly under-rated and threatened lapwing adorns the fields of the county. (DS)
BELOW: For many people the unmusical reed bunting is *the* gravel pit bird. (JW)

LEFT: The inkcap is a typical fungus of willow carr. (AG) RIGHT: Great willow herb is a plant found in marshland that fringes some gravel pits. (RHH) BELOW: Dandelions are early and showy colonisers of colliery dirt tips. (RHH)

ABOVE LEFT: Tansy is another common plant of disturbed ground. (HM) RIGHT: A male banded demoiselle found around shallow pools in gravel pit marshland. (DSm) BELOW LEFT: Surface dwelling invertebrates like this pond skater exploit the surface tension of water for their special way of life. (HM) RIGHT: The orange tip is well known for its bright colours, but this individual, feeding on garlic mustard, shows off its heavily speckled underwing. (MB)

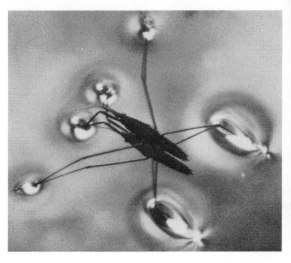

121

ABOVE: As soon as vegetation appears on dirt tips, wood mice move in to exploit the new food sources. (DW) BELOW: The short-tailed vole prefers the longer vegetation. (DW)

ABOVE: The Retford to Gainsborough railway line points towards the Clarborough Tunnel nature reserve — another link between industry and wildlife in Nottinghamshire. (MB) BELOW: Restored and unrestored sections of a dirt tip at Pye Hill Colliery. (BC)

An aerial view of perhaps the best known conservation area in Nottinghamshire — Sherwood Forest Country Park. To the south lies Edwinstowe, where legend says that Robin Hood and Maid Marion were married. Among the trees of the park is another link with Robin Hood, the equally legendary Major Oak. (NCC)

Conservation in the County

(KM)

This book has been a celebration of the birds, mammals, insects, fish and flowers of Nottinghamshire, written in grateful recognition of the pleasure and refreshment that they have provided for the people of the county over the years. However, it has also been full of the echoes of the serious problems that our wildlife faces in the modern world—of habitats under threat or lost forever, of diminished populations, of wild and romantic vistas now almost forgotten in an ever more tidy and tamed countryside. With this in mind, this final chapter is also a celebration, but this time of those people and organisations that have worked over the years to protect and conserve the wildlife of the county. In particular it celebrates the 1988 Silver Jubilee of the Nottinghamshire Trust for Nature Conservation and its twenty-five years of service to wildlife.

An interest in the flowers and creatures of the Nottinghamshire countryside is, of course, not an exclusively modern phenomenon. The county has a rich tradition of famous names going back to the days of Francis Willughby in the 17th century, W. J. Sterland in the 19th and Joseph Whitaker into the 20th. These men were great students of nature and observers of the countryside, even if their behaviour might outlaw them in the eyes of many modern conservationists. This is because their passion for nature was expressed partly through the robust pursuits of egg collecting and rarity collecting. The 'gentleman collectors' of earlier centuries (and indeed the present one) amassed huge collections of stuffed birds, especially if they were at all unusual. Joseph Whitaker's collection of birds had reached a total of 520 by the time he died in 1932 and, in addition, he also had 52 mammals. However, he also set aside 0.4 hectares (one acre) of his grounds as a bird walk, where every tree had a bird box. Hindsight might incline us to wince at the exploits of some of these early Nottinghamshire naturalists, but there is no doubt that they laid many of the foundations for today's less aggressive interest in nature. As with birds and mammals, there are also many local names that can be associated with the flora of the county. These include Dr Deering in the 18th century, Thomas Ordoyno, a nurseryman from Newark, who published a *Flora Nottinghamiensis* in 1807 and Dr Godfrey Howitt who produced a *Flora of Nottinghamshire* in 1839. Dr Howitt and his close friend Thomas Jowett were the first to appraise the botany of the county as a whole and divide it up on a geographical basis. In the first decades of the 20th century Professor John Carr brought an increasing academic rigour to the study of the county's plants, and into modern times another generation of Howitts continued the great tradition.

It is, perhaps, the founding of the Trent Valley Bird Watchers (TVBW) in 1935 that typifies the opening of the modern phase of nature conservation, in which a combination of scientific interest in and affection for wildlife has prompted so many people to work for its protection. The TVBW certainly had humble origins back in the 1930s, with seven people attending early meetings at the office of Arthur Mason, a businessman from East Bridgford. However, with advertisements for future meetings displayed in East Bridgford Post Office, and a first annual subscription of sixpence (pre-decimal, of course) agreed upon, the society gathered momentum. The celebration of its Golden Jubilee in 1985 testified to the continuing vigour of TVBW, and to the contribution that it makes to our knowledge of the birds of the county. Its eagerly awaited Annual Report, with the familiar black winged stilt emblem on the front, remains the definitive source of information on the birds of Nottinghamshire. (In 1987 TVBW changed its name to Nottinghamshire Birdwatchers.)

The Nottinghamshire Trust for Nature Conservation (hereafter 'the Trust') represents the local branch of a nationwide network of county Trusts, which now form a major element of the nature conservation movement. The first of the Trusts was founded in Norfolk in 1926, followed by Yorkshire in 1946 and Lincolnshire in 1948. With neighbours such as these, it is not surprising that interest began to develop in Nottinghamshire for a similar body. Ted Smith, from the Lincolnshire Trust, had been active during the 1950s in gingering up the county's conservationists, using the TVBW, the Nottingham and Nottinghamshire Field Club and various contacts at Nottingham University as the basis for his activities. Much discussion finally led to a meeting at Shire Hall, Nottingham, and on 4 January 1963, the Articles of Association were signed. The Trust had taken its first faltering step. The early days of a small organisation are always slightly fraught, and Margaret Price (who was Secretary of TVBW at the time as well as a founder member of the Trust) happily admits that the Trust's aims were all 'rather waffly'. A small fallow deer fawn, curled up within a frame of oak leaves, was adopted as a badge. This cuddly and appealing creature remained the figurehead until 1979 when the present, more robust, red deer stag was adopted. Arguably, the stag, being a splendid representative of an ancient species of the Nottinghamshire countryside, is a more appropriate badge than the 'imported' fallow deer. However, in those early days, the tiny fawn was, perhaps, a wise choice. Everyone needs to walk before they run.

The published purpose of the Trust was a dedication 'to the conservation of wildlife and plants, the establishment of nature reserves and advancement of research in the natural sciences'. It is perhaps worth pointing out that nature conservation in Nottinghamshire will always be of a different order to that found in counties which have, say, large areas of shoreline and estuary, or open moorland or romantic hilltop scenery upon which to capitalise. The intensively used landscape of the county might easily be overlooked in comparison. Indeed, the Trust's Annual Report for 1965 pointed out that Nottinghamshire seemed to have few sites scheduled as Sites of Special Scientific Interest (major wildlife sites) in relation to other counties. However, this kind of challenge was, and remains, an enormous spur to local conservationists, who have been keen to discover and advertise widely the precious natural features of their county.

There is no doubt that, for many people, it is the establishment of nature reserves and their management that represents the most explicit and tangible evidence of nature conservation in action. Consequently, from the earliest days of the Trust, efforts were made to seek out suitable land . At this stage the Trust was not in a position to purchase its own land, and the first reserves were managed under a variety of agreements with their owners. Examples of these were Clarbough Tunnel Top, the Fairham Brook, the roadside verge at Spalford Wood and, most important, the complex of gravel pits at Attenborough. Attenborough had been an early *cause célèbre* for local conservationists in the early 1960s, because the Central Electricity Generating Board (CEGB) had wanted to infill some of the pits with fly ash from the Ratcliffe-on-Soar Power Station. Local enthusiasts such as Dr Tony Kent and the Trust's Survey Committee argued successfully against this plan and the necessary planning permission was eventually refused to the

CEGB. This early incident, mentioned in the Trust's Annual Report for 1964, was the first of many sterling forays into the world of planning. It also set the tone for other confrontations, when important wildlife sites would come under threat. The Trust was getting its hands dirty very quickly. The immediate and desirable consequence at Attenborough was that the Trust was able to establish a good relationship with the owners and negotiate a lease with them. During 1965-66, Attenborough became Nottinghamshire's first nature reserve. The official opening on 30 April 1966 was performed by the appropriately named David Attenborough. The lease for Attenborough was, in fact, terminated in 1973, but the Trust is still involved as joint manager with Butterley Aggregates Ltd, a subsidiary of Ready Mixed Concrete plc. Attenborough remains one of the key wildlife sites in the county, especially for birds, and exemplifies some of the very best features of the gravel pit habitat.

Having established an early foothold at Attenborough, the second half of the 1960s saw the Trust expand its surveying work at important wildlife sites, and even get involved for some years in a joint educational venture with the CEGB at the Ratcliffe-on-Soar Field Studies Centre. Formal leases were obtained for a number of small sites, but the Trust had still not yet acquired any property of its own. Membership, though, had grown from 120 in 1965 to over 350 in 1970. However, the Annual Report for 1973 was able to celebrate the first freehold acquisition of land in the shape of Treswell Wood, which cost £8,900. The Chairman of the Trust at the time, John Walker, wrote '. . . Those who come to appreciate this woodland reserve in the future should remember that in a great act of faith the purchase was made with money that we did not have at the time'. A great act of faith . . . these are prophetic words which could have been repeated many times since then, and are representative of the knife-edge economics of much modern nature conservation. They also, however, reflect the enthusiasm and optimism of the conservation movement when faced by such awesome financial challenges. When the stakes are so high, and may involve the loss of a national treasure such as Treswell Wood, a way just has to be found. The Annual Report for 1973—perhaps in the same spirit of optimism—also argued that the Trust should aim 'to have 2000 members by the end of 1975, or sooner if possible'. It took, in fact, another ten years for this to be achieved.

Nature conservation in Nottinghamshire does, of course, have many elements other than the work of the Trust. Areas of land are held by a number of bodies which, although not solely dedicated to wildlife, make significant contributions to its welfare. Nottinghamshire County Council, for example, maintain Rufford Park, Sherwood Country Park and, jointly with Derbyshire, land at Creswell Crags. Nottingham City Council has also worked closely with the Trust in the development of Local Nature Reserves at Martin's Pond and Seller's Wood. The National Trust is the largest private landowner in Britain and has become a major force in nature conservation. It has few holdings in Nottinghamshire, but these do include the 1,540 hectares (3,800 acres) of Clumber Park. This important estate with its lake, its areas of woodland and open ground was created by the Dukes of Newcastle in the 18th century out of the heathland which fringed Sherwood Forest. It was bought by public subscription in 1946 and its management was taken over fully by the National Trust in 1980. It represents a substantial source of fresh air and recreation for the people of the county, as well as an important habitat for its wildlife. By a happy accident of geography, a National Trust property in Derbyshire provides a woodland site of some importance for Nottinghamshire. The Hardwick Hall estate includes one of the best woods on the Coal Measures, most of whose 12 hectares (30 acres) spill over the county boundary into Nottinghamshire.

On a smaller, but no less welcome, scale, the Woodland Trust also owns woodland in the county, including Hannah Park Wood near Worksop and Oldmoor Wood, Strelley. Birds, mammals, plants and insects can be found everywhere, but an increasing concern for nature conservation has been to identify, with an eye to protecting, the very best areas for wildlife, and to apply a special designation to them, that of Site of Special Scientific Interest (SSSI). The body responsible for this designation, and all the paperwork that goes with it, is the Nature Conservancy Council. The designation process, and the degree of protection that should be given to this relatively small number of precious places (there are just over 4,000 SSSIs) has stimulated one of the fiercest debates in modern nature conservation. Many would argue for stronger protection, especially for many SSSIs which are privately owned, while others see the whole thing as a serious interference with the rights of property. The controversy is particularly heated where the economic development of a site, for commercial or industrial purposes, may be to the detriment of the resident wildlife. The debate continues unresolved, with no copper-bottomed protection being provided for these premium sites and a deep sense of unease felt by many. In this situation, it is not surprising that SSSIs stand firmly at the top of the shopping list for every county Trust, and that the grant aid that is available to assist in nature reserve purchase is frequently dependent upon a site's designation. In Nottinghamshire there are about 56 SSSIs, all with outstanding wildlife or geological features and yet, to the continuing astonishment of many, not all are guaranteed a secure future in their present state. Besides the Trust, Nottinghamshire has a number of other organisations which study various aspects of the wildlife and countryside of the county, and do much to maintain interest in the natural world. Other natural history groups exist at Mansfield, Worksop, Wollaton and elsewhere. The Royal Society for the Protection of Birds does not have a reserve in Nottinghamshire, but active RSPB groups operate from Nottingham and Mansfield. Similarly, the county branch of the Men of the Trees Society adds its voice to the defence of the natural environment. From its headquarters at Burton Joyce, the British Trust for Conservation Volunteers runs courses in some of the practical skills required for conservation, and allows many people to get their hands and boots muddy in a good cause. Other useful 'dirty work' is done by the working parties organised by the Nottinghamshire County Council's Spadework scheme and the Nottingham Conservation Volunteers.

Over the years following the purchase of Treswell Wood, the confidence and membership of the Trust grew and in 1977 a longstanding Trust worker, Norman Lewis, was appointed as full time Conservation Officer. It was hoped that this appointment would have a coming-of-age effect on the Trust which, at the time, had a membership tantalisingly close to, but not quite, 1,000. In the event, the choice of Norman Lewis as Conservation Officer proved to be an inspired one, to the lasting benefit of the wildlife and quiet places of the county. A major project of the time, to which he became chief adviser, was the 1977/78 Biological Survey of the county. This ambitious and important project visited and documented 1,300 sites (500 of them in detail) including deciduous woodland, marsh and wet pasture, ponds and old industrial sites. 1,500 fields were looked at superficially. Each of the 1,300 sites were classified as exceptional, average or poor and the information gained overall suggested that the native wildlife of Nottinghamshire was becoming greatly reduced and fragmented. Nevertheless, the Survey, which was undertaken jointly with the Biological Records Centre of Wollaton Hall Natural History Museum, represented an enormous and vital source of information about the county, which has acted as a baseline for further research and for nature conservation initiatives and acquisitions. In the wake of all this activity, it is probably true to say that it was during the early 1980s that the Trust really got into top gear. This period witnessed spectacular increases in its holdings of important and threatened areas of land. These included ancient woods at Eaton, Gamston and Kirton, herb-rich meadows at Eakring and Teversall, and old Sherwood Forest heathland at Rainworth. Great impetus was given to this process by the Nottinghamshire Wildlife Appeal, which was launched in 1984 to raise £200,000 for reserve acquisition, to help with the cost of reserve management and to further the educational work of the Trust. This target was successfully reached at the end of 1986.

A major task of the Appeal was to obtain financial help from local people, but it is important to acknowledge that few of the Appeal's objectives (or the Trust's in general over the years) could have been achieved without the substantial help given by a wide variety of organisations. Crucial grants and loans have been provided by the Nature Conservancy Council and the World Wildlife Fund. Other financial assistance has come from the Countryside Commission, the National Heritage Memorial Fund and the Royal Society for Nature Conservation. Nottinghamshire County Council has helped with the cost of land purchase and other types of expenditure, as have the District and Parish Councils. Other donations towards conserving the nature of Nottinghamshire have come from charitable trusts, landowners and industry, the most substantial example of the latter being British Gypsum's gift to the Trust of Bunny Old Wood in 1985 and the Trust's recent association with BP at Duke's Woods.

Although the purchase and protection of the most precious areas of wildlife habitat remains the most public face of conservation, many other kinds of work remain to be done. Nature reserves, for example, run the risk of becoming rather sad and isolated 'zoos' unless work is done outside them to spread knowledge of the natural world, and to create an awareness of what must be done in other ways to assist our wildlife. Every person with a garden can become a mini-nature reserve warden with the right help and encouragement. A vigilant eye must be kept upon those who would abuse the environment through careless oversight or cynical indifference. So much to do. Much of this kind of work is done through the network of Members' Groups throughout the county which act as the eyes, ears and hands of the Trust. Through the Groups, the health and wellbeing of local wildlife can be monitored by people on the spot, and local knowledge and contacts used in its protection where possible. The Groups also provide the source for many of the talks, lectures and displays that seek to heighten public consciousness about wildlife. Throughout the year, evidence of this educational work can be seen in WI huts, draughty village halls, school classrooms, village flower shows and conservation coffee mornings all over Nottinghamshire. Education in other forms involves the Trust's fulltime staff and others in frequent contacts with the local media. Phone-in programmes, wildlife competitions and wildlife features on local radio and television have provided important opportunities to tell the conservation story. Within the constraints of time and staff available, every such opportunity is energetically seized.

Much of the image of the conservation movement involves pictures of quiet estuaries, rolling moorland or sun-dappled woods. However, it is increasingly turning its eyes towards our towns and cities as well. In 1985/86 the Trust set up the Nottingham Urban Wildlife Scheme (NUWS) with the help of a number of organisations. As a pioneering effort in the county, although there are a number of similar projects elsewhere, NUWS represents the 'rediscovery' of the urban landscape as a wildlife habitat. It also demonstrates the need to take the conservation message to urban dwellers in a form to which they can easily relate. Nature conservation may be an easy concept to grasp for those who live surrounded by a rich variety of wildlife and attractive rural scenery. It may, however, require different approaches in our urban heartland, where the wildlife may be more elusive or apparently non-existent. Nevertheless, town children as well as their country cousins should be taught to seek out and appreciate the nature of Nottinghamshire, and NUWS and its associated activities will be an exciting development in the years to come.

It is temptingly easy to look at the achievements of bodies such as the Trust and to imagine that the task of nature conservation is safe in their hands. However, this is something of a misreading of the balance of power in the countryside. A much more massive and potent influence on the future of the county's wildlife is the activity of the farming industry. Approximately 70% of Nottinghamshire is farmed as opposed to the 0.25% covered by nature reserves owned or managed by the Trust. Furthermore, it is an open secret that the relationship between the formally organised conservation movement and the farming community has not always been an entirely happy one. Conflicts have arisen over issues such as the grubbing out of hedges, the draining of wetlands and the excessive use of chemicals, to mention just a few of the most obvious ones. Fortunately, in Nottinghamshire, as elsewhere, efforts are being made to ease this relationship through the work of the Farming and Wildlife Advisory Group (FWAG). Its members are drawn from a variety of interested groups such as the Country Landowners' Association, National Farmers' Union and the Royal Society for Nature Conservation. Established in Nottinghamshire in 1977, with the enthusiastic support of the Trust, FWAG has acted as a focus for attempting to reconcile the requirements of conservation to the stern demands of the modern farming industry. Publications have been produced giving examples of good conservation practice down on the farm, such as the pamphlet about Buckwood Cottage Farm near Worksop. Other publications give advice to conservation-minded farmers on the care of hedges, trees, woodland and the variety of watery places that can be found on farms. Farmers are also encouraged to provide nest boxes for barn owls and to take a more positive view of creatures such as hawks, that may in the past have been regarded by some as 'vermin'. Interest in FWAG has been genuine and amply demonstrated by the appointment in 1984 of the first Wildlife Adviser to Nottinghamshire FWAG. The Wildlife Adviser has taken over a lot of the work that had previously been done by Norman Lewis. Much of the success or failure of nature conservation in the next 25 years will hinge upon the role played by the farming industry, and conservationists both inside and outside farming will look anxiously to FWAG and bodies like it to give a lead in pointing out the right direction. It is to be hoped that the existing trends towards conservation will quickly gather momentum.

The campaign to protect the birds, mammals, insects and plants of our countryside has been able to find no instant solutions to its problems and challenges. A spectacular reserve or two can hit the headlines from time to time, and well known television naturalists can wield a lot of beneficial influence. However, much crucial conservation work is of a more steady and routine nature. The small print of numerous planning applications needs to be scrutinised and studied for the effects that they may have on the local environment. In extreme cases objections may have to be lodged, and time-consuming submissions and public enquiries create heavy burdens for the Trust's hard-pressed fulltime staff. However, time spent poring over small print can often be as important as hours spent upon reserve management, even if it may not fit the public image of 'conservation'. A Trust Conservation Officer, for example, really does need a working knowledge of local government and the politics of conservation if he or she is to do a full job. Fortunately, many local authorities are sympathetic to conservation and enjoy good, mutual relationships with conservation bodies. This is also increasingly true of public bodies such as the Severn Trent Water Authority, which liaises closely with the Trust and seeks advice about the wildlife inplications of its various schemes.

If today presents problems and challenges, what of the future? This, of course, will involve today's children and young people and their needs are the specific responsibilty of WATCH. WATCH is the junior branch of the Trust movement and, since the mid-1980s, groups have been set up throughout Nottinghamshire. WATCH leaders, in their work with local groups and schools, seek to open the eyes of children to the joys and adventure to be found in the natural world. Much of the work is to provide the youngsters with something to do, in the belief that a morning spent pond-dipping or bird-watching on a draughty beach is a more potent teaching tool than any number of books. Much of the inspiration for the conservation movement comes from the wholesome desire to pass on to the next generation a countryside worth having. The work of WATCH contributes to this in full measure.

The task of nature conservation never stands still, and new issues continue to produce new responses. In 1985, very much in the wake of the 1981 Wildlife and Countryside Act, the Nottinghamshire Bat Group was formed to promote the welfare of these sadly misunderstood and harmless little mammals. As well as pursuing its own work, the Group also works closely with the Nature Conservancy Council in advising members of the public about bats, and in ensuring that protective legislation is observed.

The Nottinghamshire Trust for Nature Conservation has faithfully served the wildlife of the county for 25 years, and can stand back at this Silver Jubilee and briefly enjoy the fruits of its labours. As well as the influence and authority it now has, it has secured as nature reserves nearly 40 of the finest wildlife sites in the county. So, thanks to the Trust, the glorious 'green museums' of some of our best ancient woods will continue to adorn the landscape for generations to come. Thanks to the Trust, small areas of heathland which may have felt the footsteps of Robin Hood will be spared from further damage. Thanks to the Trust, wild flowers will bloom every spring in quiet pastures which have been saved from the plough.

However, the satisfaction can only be brief. The future beckons and so much remains to be done to protect what little is left of wild Nottinghamshire. Opportunities must be seized now and for this the Trust needs the money, effort, ideas, optimism and commitment of the people of the county. If you care for wildlife, join the Trust now.

Tomorrow may be too late.

A great tit is thoroughly at home in a nest box. (KM)

Nature conservation is about people as well as wildlife: LEFT: conservationists aspire to great heights in trimming back vegetation in Balloon Woods, Nottingham, (SM) and RIGHT: Cub scouts plant trees at Moorbridge Pond. (SM) BELOW: The gun goes for the start of the 1987 Run for your Wildlife race, organised by the Trust in Wollaton Park, Nottingham. Wollaton Hall is in the background. (NEP)

LEFT: Scouts work towards a conservation badge at Martin's Pond. The next generation of conservationists are already getting involved. (SM) RIGHT: Conservation involves the constant monitoring of wildlife populations: a biologist uses a pooter to collect invertebrates for study. (NTNC) BELOW: Nature reserves benefit the wildlife of the county, but they also beautify the countryside. Seen here across the fields, Eaton and Gamston Woods add charm and dignity to the horizon. (MB)

The conservation movement sets out to communicate both the beauty of nature: ABOVE: a nest of mallard ducklings (JF), and the threats that endanger it: BELOW: a badly oiled Canada goose. (M&DG)

Nottinghamshire's natural beauty: winter ice at Attenborough nature reserve. (M&DG)

Appendix I: Conservation Land in Nottinghamshire

Key

BA	Butterley Aggregates (RMC Group)	NT	National Trust
BC	British Coal	NTNC	Nottinghamshire Trust for Nature Conservation
BD	Bassetlaw District Council	NCC	Nottinghamshire County Council
BP	British Petroleum	PRI	Private owner
BR	British Rail	RB	Rushcliffe Borough Council
GB	Gedling Borough Council	TR	Tarmac Roadstone
HH	Hardys and Hansons	WFT	Winged Fellowship Trust
MD	Mansfield District Council	WT	Woodland Trust
NC	Nottingham City Council		

Access details:

★	access to members of owning/managing body or to non-members by permit	pf	public footpaths allow the public to see all or part of the reserve
★★	no access except by special permit	open	free entry at all times, please keep to the paths

NATURE RESERVES AND URBAN WILDLIFE SITES

Name	Map Ref.	Area (ha)	Owner	Manager	+ =SSSI LNR=Local nature reserve	Access
ASHTON'S MEADOW Old meadow, rich in wild flowers	SK787800	3.6	NTNC	NTNC	+	★(★★May/June)
ATTENBOROUGH GPs Mature gravel pit complex	SK521343	145.6	BA	NTNC	+	pf
BENTINCK BANKS Calcareous grassland and associated flora on old railway banks	SK491554 and SK498557	5.7	NCC	NTNC	+	★★
BRECKS PLANTATION Mixed woodland	SK554333	3.9	NC	NTNC		open
BRICKYARD PLANTATION	SK493419	0.9	WT	WT		open
BUNNY OLD WOOD Old coppiced wych elm wood	SK579283	15.3	NTNC	NTNC		open
CHILWELL MEADOW Trent Valley wet grassland	SK520356	1.0	NCC	NTNC		open
CLARBOROUGH Calcareous grassland and scrub woodland	SK756826	5.2	BR	NTNC	+	open
DANESHILL GPs Worked out gravel pits	SK666867	50.6	NCC	NTNC/NCC	LNR	open
DUKE'S WOOD Mixed deciduous woodland	SK677602	8.0	BP	NTNC	+	★
DYSCARR WOOD Primary woodland with diverse wetland plant community	SK581868	17.0	NTNC/BC	NTNC/BD	+ LNR	★part (part open)
EAKRING MEADOWS Wet meadowland and ancient hedgerow	SK702622 to SK709618	11.0	NTNC/PRI	NTNC	+	★(★★May/June)
EATON WOOD Ancient coppice woodland with interesting ground flora	SK727772	24.2	NTNC	NTNC	+	open

Name	Map Ref.	Area (ha)	Owner	Manager	+ =SSSI LNR=Local nature reserve	Access
FAIRHAM BROOK Relict lowland peat bog with reed beds and scrub	SK562338	10.5	NC	NTNC		open
FARNDON WILLOW HOLT Willow woodland and water meadows	SK767521	9.0	NTNC	NTNC		★★
FOXCOVERT PLANTATION Secondary woodland	SK587506	14.9	PRI	NTNC		★
GAMSTON WOOD Ancient coppice woodland with interesting ground flora	SK729772	40.8	NTNC	NTNC	+	★
GLAPTON WOOD Mixed woodland	SK548338	1.5	NC	NTNC		open
HANNAH PARK WOOD Remnant of northern edge of Sherwood Forest	SK590773	5.6	WT	WT		open
HARRISON'S PLANTATION A woodland site, with willow holt, rich in flora and fauna	SK530403	2.0	NC	NTNC		open
HOLLY COPSE Oak and beech woodland	SK501424	0.5	WT	WT		open
HOLME PIERREPONT GPs Wetland site for disabled birdwatchers	SK622389	9.7	TR/NCC	NTNC for WFT		★★
IDLE WASHLANDS						

The NTNC controls three areas totalling 34.8 ha, through leases or management agreements with institutional owners. As management is directed to securing them as winter refuges for wildfowl with minimum disturbance, their locations cannot be disclosed.

Name	Map Ref.	Area (ha)	Owner	Manager	+ =SSSI LNR=Local nature reserve	Access
KIMBERLEY/WATNALL CUTTING Nationally important Lower Permian geological exposure	SK498451 and SK505454	5.3	HH	NTNC	+	★
KIRTON WOOD Old ash/wych elm wood	SK708688	18.6	NTNC	NTNC	+	★
LADY LEE QUARRY Drowned quarry in magnesian limestone	SK564796	2.4	BC	NTNC		★
MARTIN'S POND Urban wetland	SK527401	4.4	NC	NTNC	LNR	pf
MEDEN TRAIL Public walkway with valuable limestone flora	SK506642 SK508648 SK527647	10.5	MD	NTNC	+/LNR	open
MOORBRIDGE POND Urban wetland site	SK547465	1.0	NC	NTNC		★★
OLDMOOR WOOD Broadleaved wood with oak and ash	SK497428	15.3	WT	WT		open
QUARRY HOLES PLANTATION Old limestone quarry with mixed woodland	SK538434	2.0	NC	NTNC		open
RAINWORTH HEATH Heathland with birch scrub	SK594591	16.0	NTNC	NTNC	+	★
SELLER'S WOOD Mixed deciduous woodland	SK525455	14.1	NC	NTNC	LNR	open
SPA PONDS Medieval and modern ponds	SK570634	6.4	PRI	NTNC		open

Name	Map Ref.	Area (ha)	Owner	Manager	+ =SSSI LNR=Local nature reserve	Access
SPALFORD WARREN Grass heathland with coniferous plantations and deciduous woodland	SK830678	36.4	NTNC	NTNC	most +	open
STAUNTON QUARRY AND WOOD Drowned Lias limestone quarry with secondary woodland	SK803458 and SK804461	3.2	PRI	NTNC		★
STONEPIT PLANTATION Mixed deciduous woodland with magnesian limestone exposure	SK514419	2.4	NTNC	NTNC		★★
TEVERSAL PASTURES Old pasture with associated flora	SK492617	5.8	NTNC	NTNC	+	★ (★★ May/June)
TRESWELL WOOD Primary ash-oak wood with hazel coppice	SK762798	47.7	NTNC	NTNC	+	★
WEST BURTON MEADOW Traditional hay meadow on ridge and furrow	SK787851	0.8	PRI	NTNC		★ (★★ May/June)
WILFORD CLAYPIT Base rich marsh plant communities and Mercia mudstone exposure	SK568356	1.2	PRI	NTNC	+/LNR	★★
WILFORD HILL WOOD Replanted woodland	SK576351	3.2	PRI	NTNC		★
WILWELL FARM CUTTING Abandoned railway line of exceptional botanical interest	SK568352	8.1	RB	NTNC	+/LNR	★

COUNTRY PARKS

Name	Map Ref	Area	Owner	Managed	SSSI	Access
BESTWOOD Grassland and woodland	SK565475	182	NCC/GB	NCC/GB		open
BURNTSTUMP Rolling parkland and woodland	SK575507	24	GB	GB		open
CLUMBER Grass, woodland, parkland and lake	SK625745	1,544	NT	NT	+	open
COLWICK Former gravel workings with lakes and woodland	SK612395	101	NC	NC		open
CRESWELL CRAGS Limestone gorge of archaeological importance with woodland	SK537744	6	PRI	NCC	+	open
LANGOLD Areas of woodland with lake	SK581865	30	BD	BD	+	open
RUFFORD Parkland, woodlands and lake	SK645655	61	NCC	NCC		open
SHERWOOD FOREST Woodland with many old oak trees	SK625675	180	PRI	NCC	+	open
WOLLATON Parkland with deer and avenue of lime trees	SK533394	222	NC	NC		open

Appendix II: Some Useful Addresses

Nottinghamshire Trust for Nature Conservation, 310 Sneinton Dale, Nottingham NG3 7DN
Nottinghamshire Birdwatchers, c/o 330 Westdale Lane, Mapperley, Nottingham
The Woodland Trust, Autumn Park, Grantham, Lincolnshire, NG31 6LL
The National Trust, Regional Office, Clumber Park Stableyard, Worksop, Nottinghamshire S80 3BE

Royal Society for the Protection of Birds, c/o 330 Westdale Lane, Mapperley, Nottingham
World Wildlife Fund Nottingham, c/o 31 Main Road, Radcliffe on Trent, Nottinghamshire
British Trust for Conservation Volunteers, Old Primary School, Burton Joyce, Nottingham
Men of the Trees Society (Notts Branch), c/o 202 Tollerton Lane, Tollerton, Nottingham
Naturalists of Wollaton, c/o 12 Spean Court, Wollaton Road, Nottingham
Langold and District Natural History Society, c/o 4 Airey Houses, Doncaster Road, Langold, Notts

FURTHER READING

DOBBS, A. (Ed). *The Birds of Nottinghamshire.* David and Charles 1975.
MORRIS, J. *Domesday Book (28) Nottinghamshire.* Phillimore, Chichester 1977.
PETERKIN, G.F. *A method for assessing woodland flora for conservation using indicator species.* Biol. Conserv. 6 239-45.
RACKHAM, O. *Trees and Woodland in the British Landscape.* Dent, 1976.
RACKHAM, O. *Ancient Woodland: its history, vegetation and uses in England.* Arnold 1980.
RACKHAM, O. *The History of the Countryside.* Dent 1986.
TYLDESLEY, D. *Birches, badgers and buttercups: Nottinghamshire's natural history.* The Cromwell Press 1986.
WEIR, C. *A prospect of Nottinghamshire.* Notts Local History Association 1986.

General Index

Figures in italics refer to illustrations.

Index
Species

1. MAMMALS

2. BIRDS

141

142

Buff-tip	*Phalera bucephala*	29
Burnet, six-spot	*Zygaena filipendulae*	60,*opp 96*
Carpet, twin spot	*Colystygia didymata*	22
Cinnabar	*Tyria jacobaeae*	*opp 49*,60
Clearwing, lunar		
hornet	*Sphecia bembeciformis*	110
Clouded buff	*Diacrisia sannio*	29
Comma	*Polygonia c-album*	22,30,110
Copper, small	*Lycaena phlaeas*	22,76,92,108
Dart, archer's	*Argrotis vestigialis*	29
shuttle-shaped	*Agrotis puta*	110
Drinker	*Philudoria potatoria*	29
Emerald, blotched	*Comibaena pustulata*	22
large	*Geometra papilionaria*	29
Gatekeeper	*Pyronia tithonus*	22,*opp 49*,60
Hairstreak, purple	*Quercusia quercus*	22,30
Hawkmoth,		
elephant	*Deilephila elpenor*	29,*opp 33,40*
poplar	*Laothoe populi*	110
Heath, small	*Coenonympha pamphilus*	76,112
Old lady	*Mormo maura*	60
Orange tip	*Anthocharis cardamines*	22,79,110,112,*121*
Painted lady	*Cynthia cardui*	22,60,*opp 96*,112
Peacock	*Inachis io*	22,30,60,79,92,95,97,112
Portland	*Ochropleura praecox*	29
Purple emperor	*Apatura iris*	30
Ringlet	*Aphantopus hyperantus*	22,108,112
Sallow, angle		
striped	*Enargia paleacea*	29
Silver lines, scarce	*Bena prasinana*	29
Silver y	*Autographa gamma*	60
Skipper, large	*Ochlodes venatus*	22,79,92,*opp 96*,112
small	*Thymelicus flavus*	22,79,92,112
Speckled wood	*Pararge argeria*	30
Swift, gold	*Hepialus hecta*	22
map-winged	*Hepialus fusconebulosa*	29
Tortoiseshell,		
small	*Aglais urticae*	22,30,60,79,92,95,97,108,112
Underwing, red	*Catocala nupta*	29
Wave, grass	*Perconia strigillaria*	29
small white	*Asthena albulata*	22
White, green-		
veined	*Artogeia napi*	22,112
large	*Pieris brassicae*	112
small	*Artogeia rapae*	22,112

5. *INSECTS OTHER THAN BUTTERFLIES AND MOTHS*

Alder fly	*Sialis lutaria*	107
Ant, black garden	*Lasius niger*	111,112
Bee, bumble	*Bombus spp*	22,92
Beetle, great diving	*Dytiscus marginalis*	107,*107*
green tiger	*Cicindela campestris*	28
sexton	*Nicrophorus vespilloides*	22
wasp	*Clytus arietis*	27
	Ampedus pomonae	28
	Ampedus pomorum	28
	Aplocnemus nigricornis	28
	Dytiscus circumcinctus	108
	Gnathoncus buyssoni	22
	Hylecoetus dermestoides	28
	Plegaderus dissectus	28
	Pterostichus oblongopunctatus	28
	Saperda scalaris	27,*opp 32*
	Strangalia spp	27
	Triplax russica	28
Bushcricket, speckled	*Leptophyes punctatissima*	22
Caddis fly	*Trichoptera*	107
Cockchafer	*Melolontha melolontha*	28
Damselfly		
bluetailed	*Ischnura elegans*	109
common azure	*Coenagrion puella*	109
common blue	*Enallagma cyathigerum*	109
demoiselle,		
banded	*Calopteryx splendens*	109,*121*
emerald	*Lestes sponsa*	109
large red	*Pyrrhosoma nymphula*	109
Devil's coachhorse	*Staphylinus olens*	112
Dragonfly		
darter, common	*Sympetrum striolatum*	109
hawker brown	*Aeshna grandis*	109
migrant	*Aeshna mixta*	109
southern	*Aeshna cyanea*	109
4-spotted chaser	*Libellula quadrimaculata*	109
Earwigs	*Dermaptera*	22
Fly, crane	*Tipulidae*	78
hover	*Syrphidae*	22,92
Glow-worm	*Lampyris noctiluca*	28
Grasshopper,		
common field	*Chorthippus brunneus*	93
Hornet	*Vespa crabro*	30
Ladybird, cream		
spot	*Calvia 14-guttata*	28
eyed	*Anatis ocellata*	28
seven spot	*Coccinella 7-punctata*	28
22 spot	*Thea 22-punctata*	28
Pond skater	*Gerris lacustris*	107,*121*
Wasp, common	*Vespula vulgaris*	22,79
Water boatman	*Notonecta glauca*	107
Water measurer	*Hydrometra stagnorum*	107
Water scorpion	*Nepa cinerea*	107,*107*

6. *INVERTEBRATES OTHER THAN INSECTS*

Mussel, swan	*Anodonta cygnaea*	107,*107*
zebra	*Dreissena polymorpha*	107
Pseudoscorpion	*Dendrochernes cyrneus*	27
Slug, tree	*Limax marginatus*	22
Snail, ramshorn	*Planorbis spp*	107,*107*
Spider:		
harvestman	*Opilio saxatoris*	111
	Araneus marmoreus	26
	Araniella cucurbitina	26
	Cyclosa conica	27
	Lepthyphantes midas	26
	Meta bourneti	26,*opp 32*
	Milliana unerrans	112
	Nuctenea umbratica	27
	Tibellus oblongus	27
	Tuberta macrophthalma	26
	Xysticus cristatus	27
	Xysticus erraticus	27
	Zora silvestris	27
Spire shells	*Hydrobia spp*	107
Sponges, freshwater	*Spongillidae*	107
Water shrimp	*Gammarus pulex*	107,*107*
Woodlouse, pill	*Armadillidium vulgare*	111

7. VASCULAR PLANTS (INCLUDES FERNS, FLOWERS, TREES AND GRASSES)

Common name	Scientific name	Pages
Adder's tongue	Ophioglossum vulgatum	79,114
Alder	Alnus glutinosa	80,93,94,109
Arrowgrass, marsh	Triglochin palustris	95
Ash	Fraxinus excelsior	19,20,21,34,39, 80,94,109
Aspen	Populus tremula	19
Balsam, Himalayan	Impatiens glandulifera	109
Bartsia, red	Odontites verna	108
Basil	Acinos arvensis	114
Beech	Fagus sylvatica	49
Bellflower, giant	Campanula latifolia	114
nettleleaved	Campanula trachelium	114
Bent, common	Agrostis tenuis	93
Bilberry	Vaccinium myrtillus	25
Bindweed	Calystegia sepium	93
Birch, downy	Betula pubescens	29
silver	Betula pendula	29,31,opp 32,94
Blackthorn	Prunus spinosa	77,84,109
Bluebell	Endymion non-scriptus	20,21,56
Bracken	Pteridium aquilinum	25,50,94
Brambles	Rubus fruticosus	22,75,92,94
Broom	Sarothamnus scoparius	75,94
Broomrape, lesser	Orobanche minor	90,91
Bryony, white	Bryonia dioica	80
Buckthorn	Rhamnus catharticus	77,80,110
Buddleia	Buddleia davidii	90,92,97
Bugle	Ajuga reptans	21
Bullace	Prunus domestica subsp institia	80
Bur-marigold	Bidens tripartita	108
Burnet, great	Sanguisorba officinalis	108
Bur-reed, branched	Sparganium erectum	107
Campion, red	Silene dioica	21
Canary grass, reed	Phalaris arundinacea	49
Cedar	Cedrus spp	49
Centaury, common	Centaurium erythraea	92,108,110,113
Chestnut, horse	Aesculus hippocastanum	94
Chestnut, sweet	Castanea sativa	49
Clover, hare's foot	Trifolium arvense	108
red	Trifolium pratense	108
Club-rush, wood	Scirpus sylvaticus	94
Cocksfoot	Dactylis glomerata	93
Coltsfoot	Tussilago farfara	91,97,111
Cornflower	Centaurea cyanus	81
Cowslip	Primula veris	21,79,87,opp 97
Crab apple	Malus sylvestris	80
Crowfoot, celery leaved	Ranunculus sceleratus	109
Currant, mountain	Ribes alpinum	114
Daisy, Michaelmas	Aster spp	92
ox-eye	Chrysanthemum leucanthemum	79,93,111
Dandelion	Taraxacum officinale	111,120
Dock, golden	Rumex maritimus	110
great water	Rumex hydrolapathum	109
Dog's-tail, crested	Cynosurus cristatus	93
Dogwood	Thelycrania sanguinea	21
Duckweed, common	Lemna minor	95
ivy	Lemna trisulca	95
Elder	Sambucus nigra	56,75,80,92,109,110,
Elm	Ulmus spp	19,77,80
Fennel	Foeniculum vulgare	90,92
Fescue, barren	Vulpia bromoides	93
rat's tail	Vulpia myorus	91
red	Festuca rubra	93
Figwort, water	Scrophularia aquatica	109
Flag, sweet	Acorus calamus	49,52
yellow	Iris pseudacorus	110,opp 113
Flax, purging	Linum catharticum	113
Fleabane, Canadian	Conyza canadensis	91
Forget-me-not, water	Myosotis scorpioides	109
Foxglove	Digitalis purpurea	94,23,99
Garlic, crow	Allium vineale	108
Wood	Allium ursinum	56
Goat's-beard	Tragopogon pratensis	111
Golden rod	Solidago virgaurea	92
Goose grass	Galium aparine	94
Gorse	Ulex europaeus	75
Grass, oat	Arrhenatherum elatius	93
quaking	Briza media	93
sweet vernal	Anthoxanthum odoratum	93
wavy-hair	Deschampsia flexuosa	93
Gypsywort	Lycopus europaeus	49,110
Hair-grass, silver	Aira caryophyllea	91
Harebell	Campanula rotundifolia	26,93,108
Hawthorn	Crataegus monogyna	28,56,75,79,80, 92
woodland	Crataegus oxyacantha	20,38
Hayrattle	Rhinanthus minor	79
Hazel	Corylus avellana	19,20,21,25,80
Helleborine, broad leaved	Epipactis helleborine	22,94,98
Hemlock	Conium maculatum	108
Hemp agrimony	Eupatorium cannabinum	110
Herb paris	Paris quadrifolia	20,23,32
Holly	Ilex aquifolium	25,75,80
Honeysuckle	Lonicera periclymenum	21
Horsetail, marsh	Equisetum palustre	79,94
water	Equisetum fluviatile	94
wood	Equisetum sylvaticum	94
Hound's tongue	Cynoglossum officinale	49
Ivy	Hedera helix	93
Japanese knotweed	Polygonum cuspidatum	91
Juniper	Juniperus communis	19
Knapweed, great	Centaurea scabiosa	111
Lady's smock	Cardamine pratensis	79,opp 97
Lesser celandine	Ranunculus ficaria	60,68
Lime	Tilia x europaea	49
Lime, small-leaved	Tilia cordata	19,20,25
Loosestrife, purple	Lythrum salicaria	opp 48,60,109,110
Maple, field	Acer campestre	21,77,80
Marigold, corn	Chrysanthemum segetum	81
marsh	Caltha palustris	79
Marjoram	Origanum vulgare	114
Meadow sweet	Filipendula ulmaria	109,110
Melick, wood	Melica uniflora	20
Melilot, common	Melilotus officinalis	91
Mercury, dog's	Mercurialis perennis	20,21
Mint, water	Mentha aquatica	94,109
Mustard, garlic	Alliaria petiolata	121
hedge	Sisymbrium officinale	91
Nettle, stinging	Urtica dioica	94,108
Nightshade, woody	Solanum dulcamara	80
Oak	Quercus spp	19,21,25,26, 27,28,29,30, 31,48,49,50, 75,80,92,94, 114
pedunculate	Quercus robur	94

Orchid, bee	*Ophrys apifera*	*opp 113*,114
butterfly	*Plantanthera chlorantha*	22,*opp 32*
common spotted	*Dactylorhiza fuchsii*	79,110
early purple	*Orchis mascula*	22,*34*
green-winged	*Orchis morio*	*opp 113*,114
pyramidal	*Anacamptis pyramidalis*	114
Osier	*Salix viminalis*	109,110
Oxlip, false	*Primula veris x*	
	vulgaris	79
Parsley, cow	*Anthriscus sylvestris*	93
Pea, everlasting	*Lathyrus latifolius*	114
Pear, wild	*Pyrus communis*	80
Persicaria	*Polygonum persicaria*	108
Petty Whin	*Genista anglica*	25,*42*
Pine, Scots	*Pinus syvestris*	19,28,49
Plantain, water	*Alisma*	
	plantago-aquatica	107,109
Pondweed, broad-		
leaved	*Potamogeton natans*	107
Poplar, black	*Populus nigra*	109
Poppy, common	*Papaver rhoeas*	73,81,*81*,91,108
Primrose	*Primula vulgaris*	*33*,56,79,*opp*
		96
common evening	*Oenothera biennis*	91
Privet	*Ligustrum vulgare*	80
Ragged robin	*Lychnis flos-cuculi*	79,*87*,94,95,110
Ragwort	*Senecio jacobaea*	*opp 49*,111
Oxford	*Senecio squalidis*	91,114
Reed, common	*Phragmites communis*	49,115
Reedmace	*Typha latifolia*	49,62,94,95,107,115
lesser	*Typha angustifolia*	95,109
Restharrow	*Ononis repens*	93
spiney	*Ononis spinosa*	114
Rocket, annual		
wall	*Diplotaxis muralis*	90,91
Rose, dog	*Rosa canina*	77,80,*84*,92
field	*Rosa arvensis*	77,80,*85*
Rose, guelder	*Viburnum opulus*	56,*65*,80
Rowan	*Sorbus aucuparia*	25
Rush, flowering	*Butomus umbellatus*	109
soft	*Juncus effusus*	115
Sallow (goat		
willow)	*Salix caprea*	77,109,114
Scented woodruff	*Galium odoratum*	20

Scentless mayweed	*Tripleurospermum*	
	inodorum	91
Sedge, false fox	*Carex otrubae*	94,107
greater tussock	*Carex paniculata*	49
pendulous	*Carex pendula*	107,*117*
remote-flowered	*Carex remota*	95
Skull-cap	*Scutellaria galericulata*	49,94
Sorrel, common	*Rumex acetosa*	79
sheep's	*Rumex acetosella*	108
wood	*Oxalis acetosella*	20,*32*
Spurge, cypress	*Euphorbia cyparissias*	114
St John's wort	*Hypericum perforatum*	108
Stitchwort, greater	*Stellaria holostea*	21,56
Sweet grass, reed	*Glyceria maxima*	62,107
Sycamore	*Acer pseudoplatanus*	21,49,94
Tansy	*Chrysanthemum vulgare*	60,108,*121*
Teasel	*Dipsacus fullonum*	76,92,111
Thistles	*Cirsium spp*	28,76,79,92
marsh	*Cirsium palustre*	108
spear	*Cirsium vulgare*	108
Toadflax, common	*Linaria vulgaris*	114
ivy-leaved	*Cymbalaria muralis*	90
Pale	*Linaria repens*	114
Traveller's joy	*Clematis vitalba*	114
Trefoil, bird's-foot	*Lotus corniculatus*	60,111
Violet, common	*Viola riviniana*	21,*36*,79
Water-cress	*Rorippa nasturtium-*	
	aquatica	94
Water dropwort,	*Oenanthe fistulosa*	109
common		
fine-leaved	*Oenanthe aquatica*	109
Wellingtonia	*Sequoiadendron*	49
	giganteum	
Wild angelica	*Angelica sylvestris*	94
Wild service	*Sorbus torminalis*	20,21,*32*
Willow, crack	*Salix fragilis*	94,109
white	*Salix alba*	109,114
Willowherb, great	*Epilobium hirsutum*	60,109,*120*
rosebay	*Chamaenerion*	
	angustifolium	29,91,92,114
Wood anemone	*Anemone nemorosa*	20,21,*opp 96*
Wood sage	*Teucrium scorodonia*	94
Yellow archangel	*Galeobdolon luteum*	20,21,56,*65*
Yellow-wort	*Blackstonia perfoliata*	91,113,114
Yorkshire fog	*Holcus lanatus*	93

8. NONVASCULAR PLANTS (ALGAE, LIVERWORTS, MOSSES, FUNGI)

Bryophytes		110
Fungus, bracket	*Fistulina hepatica*	28,*39*
	Laetiporus sulphureus	28,*39*
	Piptoporus betulinus	28,*39*
Ink cap, shaggy	*Coprinus comatus*	110,*120*
Jew's ear	*Auricularia auricula*	
	judae	92,110

Lichen spp	*Candelariella vitellina*	90,91
	Xanthoria parientina	90
Milk cap, saffron	*Lactarius deliciosus*	92
Miller, the	*Clitopilus prunulus*	92
Russula, bare toothed		
	Russula vesca	92

Subscribers

Presentation Copies

1 **Nottinghamshire Trust for Nature Conservation**
2 **Sir David Attenborough CBE FRS**
3 **Royal Society for Nature Conservation**
4 **Nature Conservancy Council**
5 **Nottinghamshire County Council**
6 **Nottinghamshire County Leisure & Recreation Services**

7 Richard Marquiss
8 Clive & Carolyn Birch
9 David N. Robinson
10 Nottinghamshire Trust for
17 Nature Conservation
18 Mrs E.G. Gilbert
19
20 H.W Palin
21 Mrs E.E Keefe
22 James A. Wright
23 J.D Winn
24 Sarah Mason
25 Miss Karen L. Buckley
26 Jenni Coe
27 A.W. Green
28 Dr Michael E. Archer
29 Mrs S.M. Swift
30 M.J. Hill
31 Michael John Cox
32 A.S. Gilbert
33 Dr P.G. Dodsworth
34 R.G. Bacon
35 F.G. Munday
36 H. Revill
37 C. Clements
38 Margaret Harris
39 Victoria & Albert Museum
40 Derek Wilkinson
41 Muriel Parkinson
42 John Brian Betts
43 Mrs Jane Iliffe
44 Brian Terence Lane
45 Andrew Goodall
46 John O. Lane
47 Trisha Phillips
48 G.H. Brierley
49 Mrs J.V. Thompson
50 Ramon Frank Green
51 T.M. Pepper
52 Mrs G.B. Pepper
53 R.T. McAndrew
54 P.J.M. Nethercott
55 David Corke
56 Ivy & Alan Organ
57 Thomas F.G. Stocker
58 Joy Staples
59 Mr & Mrs G. Stanley
60 Dr C.J. Stanley

61 R. Dent
62 Jack Oliver
63 E.E. Lawrence
64 Andrew David Powers
65 Mr & Mrs F. Hudson
66 A.K. Kent
67
69 Mr & Mrs A. Harwood
70 People's College of FE,
Nottingham
71 Tim & Gail Chamberlain
72 Anthony E. Riddle
73 J.R. Davies
74 M. Winifred Slight
75 Trent Polytechnic,
Nottingham
76 Eileen M. Curtiss
77 Martin Catt
78 Clare & Mark Kitchen
79 Audrey & Arthur Grindley
80 T.E. Deeming
81 Ken Dawson
82 Miss D.A. Phillips
83 Wyn Harvey
84 John W. Everett
85 Dr F.K. Hammond
86 Mrs J. Anderson
87 Vaughan Wayne Beardsley
88 Joan Strutt
89 J. Reeks
90 Mrs Sheila M. Williams
91 Derek Edmundson
92 Mrs Sheila Harris
93 Mary & John Morley-Kirk
94 Margarette Barwick
95 P. Webb
96 Kenneth Smith
97 Colin G. Lamb
98 Harry Frith
99 Rita A. Cope
100 Susan Holmes
101 E.H. Roberts
102 Ms M.A. Poole
103 A.E. Davis
104 Mrs S. Millar
105 Miss D. Glover
106 D. Fielden
107 Miss K.M. Smith

108 J. Tidmarsh
109 Edith W. Sands
110 D.J.W. Usher
111 A.R. Stone
112 D. Heffernan
113
114 Miss C.M. Ford
115
116 W.M. Wright
117 E.D. Beesley
118 K. Wood
119 Mrs H.A. Silvester
120 M.T. Weston
121 Kenneth Bray
122 J.W. Halford
123 A.W. Bull
124 C.J. Pursglove
125 I.K. Dawson
126 Colin D. Newlands
127 Peter E. Maggs
128 Dr G.H.R. Curnock
129 P.J. Marks
130 R.C. Malinsky
131 R.J. Collier
132 The Natural History
Museum, Wollaton
133 Brian Playle
134 Sheila M. Elsdon
135 Miss Debra Abbott
136 N.D. Collier
137 Henry Sampey Blagg
138 R.I. Adams
139 A.D. Cox
140 Alan & Jill Watson
141 Edward T. Jackson
142 Annette Evans
143 Miss S. Mackie
144 Dr Nicholas Seivewright
145 E. Cowley
146 Marjorie Heath Benson
147 Dr D.H. Bowen
148 J. Curtain
149 Jessie Doreen Dunford
150 Mrs Rachel Leah
151 Miss M.E. Price
152 Ms Tina Porcheret
153 David Robert Smith
154 Allen Wood

155 Miss T.G. Forrow
156 Dai Hayes
157 Gareth & Jenny Parsons
158 Miss P.S. Taylor
159 David Brown
160 A. Barnes
161 Patricia Greene
162 Mr & Mrs L.V. Proctor
163 Martin Brownett
164 Ralph Potton
165 Forestry Commission
166 Norman Shelley
167 Dr H.A. Buck
168 Mrs J. Hardy
169 Mrs R.R. Bundy
170 Peter Sadler
171
172 Margaret Birkinshaw
173 J. Gurnhill
174 Mr & Mrs J.B. Hutchinson
175 Victor Brett
176 Jeffrey Noble
177 Mr & Mrs S. Eyre
178 John W. Eaton
179 L. Bullimore
180 R. Bradshaw
181 Jane Bennett
182 Miss D. Kelly
183 Anthony David Wood
184 Mrs M.I. Wale
185 D.A. Burgess
186
187 J.G. Smart
188 A.E. Denker
189 S.C. Knight
190 Dr A.R. Anderson
191 Mrs N. Stephenson
192 Mrs A. Lees
193
194 Mary Ruth Leach
195 Shireen Neely
196 J. Jackson
197 F.A. Pickett
198 C.A. Barton
199 Dr C.R. Salisbury
200 Michael C. Powell
201 P. Simpson
202 J.M. Iles

203 Mr & Mrs I.M. Campbell	268 Miss M. Hampton	335 Ms A. Oswin	414 R. Trease
204 Elizabeth & Frank Leaver	269 G.T. Harlow	336	415 Mrs J. Sadler
205 B. Cooper	270 I. Hopper	337 Christine A.M. Ross	416 B.J. Cast
206 Doreen Silvester	271 Miss B.E. Smith	338 A.C. Gill Ltd	418
207 Patricia A. Hewis	272 Miss B. Croshaw	357	419 Carol Collins
208 J.F. Rands	273 Mrs D. Smith	358 Tony Nelson	420 Miss B.C. Hampson
209 John Holmes	274 W.J. Turton	359 M.J. & L.K. Redfearn	421 Mrs G.A. James
210 Philip Lyth	275 C. King	360 J.W. Wholey	422 M.E. Ward
211 K.R. Harrop	276 T.S. Nutting	361 R.L. Johnson	423 D. Thompson
212 K. Holland	277 A.H. Carruthers	362 Joe & Elizabeth Mardel-Ferreira	424 Mrs S.A. Bramley
213 Paul J. Newton	278 R.T. Sears		425 Glyn Jones
214 Jill E. Clarke	279 Mrs P.D. Waite	363 Roger & Ileana McMeeking	426 Ralph Sorrell
215 J.R. McB. Allan	280 Alan R. Watson		427 Roy Edmunds
216 P.D. Dickin	281 D.A. Woolder	364 Winard & Maria Klein	428 Roger A. Kirk
217 Mrs J. Thomas	282	365 Anne-Christine Strugnell	429 June Marshall
218 Brian Tidy	283 Dr P.G. Smith	366 Duncan & Elsie MacConachie	430 Frank W. Merrin
219 V. Gibson	284 Roy Brooksbank		431 L.A. Saunders
220 David Newman	285 H.A. Green	367 Mary McMeeking	432 John L. Griffiths
221 Paul Morrison	286 Alan Crich	368 Angus McMeeking	433 Trevor John Wright
222 Tom Myall	287 C.W. Elston	369 Alasdair & Kirsteen Lewis	434 Michael Parkin
223 Peter Kenneth York	288	370 Duncan & Ruth McMeeking	435 Mrs Teresa Anne Benham
224 R.I. Heppenstall	289 T.H. Payne		436 Margaret Spolton
225 B.A. Hopkinson	290 R.S.T. Hampshire	371 John M. McMeeking	437 Nancy Tallents
226 Neil M.G. Shepperson	291 Dr J.K. Bingham	372 Mrs J. Panton	438 R.G. Piper
227 Malcolm Andrew Smith	292 Ray Bickel	373 A. Henshaw	439 Arthur D. Cummins
228 Mrs P.M. Keeton	293 Mrs C. Strong	374 Mrs N. Wright	440 Miss B. Raynor
229 June Ortlieb	294 Ken Elliott	375 Kenneth Eric Martin	441 I.D.P. Thorne
230 D.M. Huskisson	295 Martin Roberts	376 R.I. Heppenstall	442 Geoffrey Pearson MBE
231 Mrs Enid M. Sutton	296 J.D. Smith	377 Mrs E. Kipping	443 Anthony Harwick Wilkinson
232 Dr Patrick Harding	297 J.E. Richmond	378 Mrs A. Stainforth	
233	298 Paula R. Thompson	379 D. Breeze	444 K.P. Roadley
234 Brian Davies	299 Ian Paul Overton	380 Mrs S.C. Stevenson	445 James R. Todd
235 K.J. Orpe	300 Christopher Watkinson	381 Mrs J.A. Axtell	446 Anthony C.M.B. Scott
236 Andrew W. Mason	301 Peter Gary Button	382 R. Horobin	447 John Saint
237 J.R. Fletcher	302 C.H.J. Dredge	383 Mrs N. Tongue	448 S.G. Drew
238 Bernard Ellis	303 A. Newman	384 D. Holt	449 Graham C. Jukes
239 Sheila D. Nourse	304 Dr Michael E. Archer	385 Mrs S. Lane	450 S.A. Gilbert
240 Harold Gudgin	305 Ian & Sue Dunn	386 Dr G.B. Wilson	451 Michael John Webster
241 J.R. Whitfield	306 F.E. Challands	387 B. Harling	452 Andrew Burns
242 Rowland Widdison	307 Kenneth E. Adams	388 Miss M. Bryant	453 J.D. Wall
243 David Haynes	308 F. Harrison	389	454 M.R. Lucas
244 P.L. O'Malley	309 Mrs M.J. Gillham	390 Dr A.M. Birch	455 R.P. Fletcher
245 Mrs A. Mitchell	310 Mrs S.M. Martin	391 M.C. Bryant	456 T.H.B. Bowles
246 M. Mounteney	311	392 Christine T. Kettles	457 Dr Nigel de Gay
247 Helen Mitchell	312 John Gerard de Nobriga	393	458 Alan G. Lewis
248 G. Woolley	313 Richard Marquiss	394 R.H. Nurcombe	459 Mrs W.D. Parsons
249 George Flint	314 P. Shepherd	395 R.G.S. Blades	460 Keith Andrew Sampson
250 Miss A.M Brock	315 R. Cobb	396 D.C. Catchpole	461 Marjorie Campion
251 Richard Marquiss	316 D.W. Johnson	397 D.J. Radford	464
252 Mr & Mrs L. Marquiss	317 C. David Edgar	398 Mr & Mrs W.R. Ball	465 Norma Braithwaite
253 Mr & Mrs B.G. Dodgson	320	399 D.S. Willis	466 Gordon MacGregor
254 M.R. Bartle	321 Lynda Milner	400 John Boseley	467 Mary Sterland
255 R. Withers	322 Victoria Bealby	401 A.K. Latchetta	468
256 D.J. Alton	323 Helen R. Bealby	402 Brenda J. Cox	469 Mrs E.M. Lawson
257 Reverend S.F. Rising	324 Gavin P. Walker	403 Miss S. King	470 E. Brearley
258 Mrs J.M. Bartle	325 Meirion L. Walker	404 J.K. Adams	471 Keith H. Hill
259 M. Walpole	326 Barbara J. Walker	405	472 Mary & Malcolm Stacey
260 Mrs B. Sissons	327 D. Hammocks	406 Mr & Mrs T.B. Fleetham	473 M.D. Grant
261 R.D. Milnes	328 Mrs J.M. Fairhurst	407 A.P. Brady	474 Mrs M.M. Page
262	329 Mary Rose Johnstone	408 R.S. Brown	475 George Henry Paris
263 Mrs L. Randle	330 Miss S.P. Hallam	409 Mrs G.M. Skellington	476 Andrew Ronald Paris
264	331 Colin Timothy Bickerstaffe	410 Julie P. Palmer	477 Mrs V. Olifent
265 Mrs F.M. Gardiner	332 John Lucas	411 P.G. Phillips	478 H.E.C. Toft
266 Mrs H.E. Dobbs	333 M.C. Prout	412 G.S. Ritchie	479 Mrs E.M. Wells
267 Mr & Mrs J.R. Jackson	334 Valerie Hunt	413 Mrs N. Ratcliffe	480 Joyce & Tony Riding

481 Paul Nichol BSc MPhil
482 John M. Hurst
483 D.R. Warren
484 Mrs H.M. Menzies
485 J.A. Firth
486 Lady Whitaker
487 Dr R.C. Wilson
488 J.P.C. Burgess
489 R.W.D. Hanson
490 Michael R. Wallace
491
492 Colin M. Bowler
493 L.P. Martin
494 B. Irene Jones
495 K.R. Screen
496 Mrs A.M. Phillips
497 Sydney Barnes
498 Sheila McMullan
499 Notts Farming & Wildlife
    Advisory Group
500 Alan Field
501 P. Carter
502 Mrs J. Collins
503 M.O. Winfield
504 E. Adams
505 J. Cross
506 J. Crocker
507 R.A. Mills
508 Heidi Ames
509
510 Lady Lorna Kent
511 Mrs A. Lynd-Evans
512 Prof K.W.H. Stevens
513 J.E. Osborne
514 Julie M. Straw
515 G.C. Reed
516 Mrs J.D. Bishop
517 C.D. Pons
518 Mrs A.D. Norman
519 Miss J. Marriott
520 A.A. Smith
521 N.A. Taylor
522 Local Studies Library,
545 Nottingham
546
548 D.H. Tyldesley
549 Miss M. Smith
550 J.D. Ellis
551 R. Poppleton
552
553 T.H. Payne
554 R.H. Wilson
555 K. Orpe
556 Dr A.C. Warne
557 I.G. Solly
558 P. Bowler
559 F. Harrison
560 M.J. Roberts
561 M. Webb
562 F.K. Sterland
563 Mrs J.G. Moss
564 Keith Streb
565 Jean Wheatcroft

566 Steve Whiteley
567 Dr Brendan Jacobs
568 Sarah Montgomery
569 Alison Betts
570 J.M. Needham
571 B.L. Traini
572 Malcolm G. Fisher
573 Mrs M. Shaw
574
575 Martin Davies
576 Miss F.N. Mulholland
577 Brian W. Wetton
578 Mrs G.L. Allen
579
580 Jim Whitby
581 Anne Hughes
582 Nottinghamshire County
585 Council
586 Paul Wright
587 Dr Jack Rieley
588 N.R. Lewis
589 Mrs M.J. Braithwaite
590 Graham Page
591 N.D. Collier
592
593 Mrs Dodsworth
594 Mrs J.T. Sansom
585 John T. Robertson
596 Hugh Miller
597 Michael J. Barke
598 Giles Darvill
599 J.O. Knight
600 Mrs B. Baggaley
601
620 Nottinghamshire County
    Council
621 John L. Muncey
622 David Swan
623 A. Hughes
624 R. Eminson
625 R.J. Ayers
626 B.D. Suter
627 P. Read
628 John Martin Leadley
629 J.M. Nicholson
630 M.K. Chilvers
631 Mrs M. Holden
632 Brenda J. Cox
633 P. Hull
634 Ian David Gates
635 L. & J. Otterstrom
636 Mrs B. Leach
637 Mrs E. Cordall
638 Mrs S.E. Piper
639 M. Klimek
640 Miss Margaret Hill
641 A.A. Edmans
642 Meredith Lawrence
643 E. Bettinson
644 Mrs R.M. Cooper
645 Mr & Mrs T.R. Oxley
646 A.G. Gough
647 A. Hudson

648 J.R.F. Jackson
649 Mrs L.N. Wain
650 Mrs A.M. Gregory
651 Miss J. Cherry
652 Mrs Mary A. Howard
653 Ronald Askew
654 Mrs Patricia Woods
655 Dr E.B. Knight-Jones
656 Mrs Margaret Toule
657 Judith Edgar
658 A.R.E. Houldsworth
659 Denis Worthington
660
661 J.R. Booth
662 J.D.W. Coales
663 Dr C.B. Wain
664 Dorothy J. Herlihy
665 Colin Green
666 David A. Horobin
667 Roy A. Frost
668 Martin Smith
669 Greg Smith
670 John Wilson
671 Miss J.S. Kendrick
672 James R. Freeman
673 Mr & Mrs J.M. Clark
674 Keith N.A. Alexander
675 Alan J.F. Drayton
676 M.J. Baghurst
677 Ron Matthews
678 Paul Bingham
679 David Dwelly
680 Mrs A.M. Hickling
681 Drew Cope
682 J.F. Parsons
683
684 Miss B. Furley
685 Dr B.D. Wheeler
686 Terence Balchin
687 D. Herringshaw
688 G.R. Golder
689 Stella C. Browne
690 Arthur East
691 Dr Ian D. Rotherham
692 Kathleen M. Kinsey
693 D.M. Bednall
694 Mrs Hilary A. Silvester
695 John W. Wilson
696 Brian Yates
697 T.E. Harper
698 Ann M. Hodgkinson
699 Graham Sharpe
700 Mrs K.S. Pressland
701 James Tandy
702 R. Young
703 G.W. Russell
704 M.E. Caunt
705 G. Caunt
706 R.H. Jones
707 Miss Gladys Pickford
708 G. Layer
709 Cathy Sellars
710 V.L. Holt

711 John M. Gill
712 Mrs M.A. Woodhead
713 Elizabeth Clough
714 Mrs S. Beardall
715 Kathleen E. Smith
716 C.A. Barton
717 R.S. Copestake
718 Frank Poizer
719 Trevor Poizer
720 Mr & Mrs W.E. Shaw
721 Robert B. Brown
722 G.J. Smart
723 Veronica Belton
724 P.G. Phillips
725 Joan Walker
726 Ms N. Holmes ·
727 Keith John Corbett
728
731 Lincolnshire Library
    Service
732
733 Leicestershire Libraries &
    Information Service
734 David J. Glaves
735 John P. Dyson
736 R.G.N. Bird
737 Nottinghamshire County
    Council Leisure Services
738 Barbara Perry
739 Leslie R. & Susan Frost
740 John Temple
741 Rosemary Jordan
742 Dr Alan Wilmot
743 Godfrey Fry
744 T.W. Cupit
745 Margaret Standring
746 Mrs Joyce Beidas
747
748 Derick Scott
749 D. Budworth
750 Dr G.S. Bowpitt
751 Alan A. Smith
752 S.E. Adcock
753 M.J. Stacey
754 R.J. Braithwaite
755 D.G. Martin
756 James William Halford
757 Miss J.F. King
758 John E. Morley
759 Patricia Greene
760 Malcolm David Pool
761 Graham Allen
762 Peter Mokes
763 Ian & Jennifer Duce
764 Joan Olko
765 Mrs Marjorie Field
766 Frank Noonan & Tina
    Porcheret
767 R.B. Powell
768 Mrs L.M. Brookes
769 Mrs Denise Sellick
770 K.E. Giles
Remaining names unlisted

N.T.N.C. Nature Reserves & Urban Wildlife Sites

1. Wilwell Farm Cutting
2. Fairham Brook
3. Attenborough Gravel Pits
4. Martin's Pond
5. Stonepit Plantation
6a. Kimberley Cutting
6b. Watnall Cutting
7. Seller's Wood
8. Foxcovert Plantation
9. Lady Lee Quarry
10. Dyscarr Wood
11. Idle Washlands
12. West Burton Meadow
13. Clarborough Tunnel
14. Treswell Wood
15. Spalford Warren
16. Eakring Meadows
17. Staunton Quarry
18. Holme Pierrepont Gravel Pit
19. Wilford Clay Pit
20. Bentinck Banks
21. Gamston Wood
22. Eaton Wood
23. Teversal Pastures
24. Meden Trail
25. Spa Ponds
26. Kirton Wood
27. Daneshill Gravel Pits
28. Rainworth Heath
29. Ashton's Meadow
30. Duke's Wood
31. Bunny Old Wood
32. Wilford Hill Wood
33. Chilwell Meadow
34. Farndon Willow Holt and Water Meadows
35. Moorbridge Pond
36. Harrison's Plantation
37. Quarry Holes Plantation
38. Glapton Wood
39. Brecks Plantation

■ Country Parks

1. Bestwood
2. Rufford
3. Sherwood Forest
4. Cresswell Crags
5. Clumber Park
6. Colwick
7. Wollaton Park
8. Burntstump
9. Langold

◆ Woodland Trust Reserves

1. Oldmoor Wood
2. Brickyard Plantation
3. Holly Copse
4. Hannah Park Wood
5. Jacklin's Wood

Calverton

Hucknall